Silver

SILVER

An Illustrated Guide to Collecting Silver
by Margaret Holland

PEERAGE BOOKS

First published in Great Britain by Octopus Books Limited
This edition published by Peerage Books
59 Grosvenor Street
London W1

© 1973 Octopus Books Limited

Reprinted 1983

ISBN 0 907408 24 9

Printed in Hong Kong

PREVIOUS PAGE *a George II kettle, lamp and stand by Robert Tyrrell; 1752*

THIS PAGE *a teapot by Zachariah Bryden, Boston; 1760*

FOLLOWING PAGES *sugar bowls, cream pitcher and teapot with tray by Paul Revere; American c 1770*

Contents

ESSE QUAM VIDERI

A Background to Collecting Silver

BEAKERS · NUTMEG GRATERS · BUTTONS · PEACE MEDALS · AMERICAN PORRINGERS

It was many centuries before the birth of Christ that silver was first fashioned into objects for adornment and use. Even at that time its value was recognized, and countries without this precious metal felt their sailors were justified in attempting the capture of silver-bearing ships from those that mined it, a sport that continued almost to modern times. For instance American privateers raided Mexican ships until 1860, when mines were discovered in America itself, which then became the leading producer. Silver is rarely mined as such but is extracted from lead, copper and, to a lesser extent, other ores. In the early days England, which got its main supplies from Germany or Spain, also produced a modicum of silver from the lead mines dotted around Scotland, Wales and Northern England.

The possession of silver became a yard-stick of real wealth. Only very few were able to establish their position by having such things as eating bowls or spoons of silver (which were normally produced in wood, horn or base metals). It was also a form of investment, and although intricate decoration on articles may have added to their snob value, silver was for centuries considered only as we consider money in the bank, earning its keep by being useful in the meantime. That is why so little early silver survives; if it was not demanded as a tax, levied to pay for wars or a ruler's extravagance, then it could be sold by the owner who had kept it against a rainy day. If no such need arose it would be melted down

and re-fashioned when he was able to afford it – for to be up to date was always important. Quantities of old English and Dutch silver were taken to America by the early settlers and used to tide them over their first years there. Only a little of this found its way to the workshops of the first silversmiths in New England such as Robert Sanderson (1608–93) who started work in Boston in 1634, to provide the metal for America's first dram cups, tankards, and beakers. The earliest beakers at first followed the Scottish style and were used, as were those north of the River Tay, in both home and church. The survival of the early pieces in such conditions was largely a matter of luck, though one likes to imagine that where a choice existed, it was the less impressive piece that went into the pot to provide plate (a word that covers all silver objects as opposed to bullion or coin) in the new fashion.

It is small wonder that the earliest American work has a high scarcity value, although something like 150 silversmiths had been established in Boston by 1800. About a generation after work had started in Boston, goldsmiths set up in New York, where both their names and the styles they produced were Dutch, and in Philadelphia around 1690 the first craftsman set about fulfilling the orders of wealthy Quakers, who liked quality without frills. (Goldsmith was a general term which embraced silversmiths.)

On the whole, styles in America followed those in England (which were also largely taken from the Continent and then anglicized). The American craftsmen perhaps continued to make the old forms somewhat longer than the English, although the more enterprising among them worked out new forms. There are, however, plenty of exceptions even when

LEFT a beaker in the Dutch style by Hull and Sanderson, Boston; 1760. The crest, motto and handle were added later totally ruining the balance

ABOVE *a beaker by Paul Revere*

RIGHT *a German silver-gilt beaker by S. B. Ferrn, Nurenburg; second half 17th century*

one omits New York's early Dutch-inspired silver made before the Queen Anne period. By that time much that is grand, but not collectable, in English silver had been created, and largely destroyed. In England, at any time, there was more 'special' silver made, where the courts, ancestral homes and ambassadors travelling abroad, all needed prestige wares. There were also many more craftsmen, working for a community that included more rich people, but while American goldsmiths worked scrupulously to standards and needed no supervision, the same could not be said for those in England where a method of search and trial, called the assay, was necessary.

Because of this the hallmarking system came about, but the marks stamped upon silver were never intended to benefit any but those concerned with the enforcement of law in England, even though today they can be read like a history book. They are of the greatest help in the identification of such silver, particularly to the beginner, but the real expert will regard them as a check point rather than the last word on the subject. Understanding marks is worth little compared to a knowledge of silver itself, gained by experience and time spent studying museum and fine private collections. It is only by looking at the best available work that one's judgement is formed

and the collector whose interests are confined to his own price range is doomed to failure.

Many of the points the expert will see at a glance will be discussed in context, but others depend on an inner eye and cannot adequately be put into words. The beginner may see two bowls as identical, yet there will be a difference in price that only an expert understands. One bowl is superior in every way and the expert knows it because practice has developed his eye, although he may be quite unable to explain its elusive quality. As knowledge grows so does satisfaction and when the beginner, entering a shop, sees both a Queen Anne coffee pot and its faithful reproduction, made in quantity during the nineteenth century, and knows for the first time which is which, an immense thrill is experienced. Later he will wonder how he ever mistook one for the other for, to the experienced eye, the colour is totally different and a richly glowing outer skin called the patina, formed over the centuries, proclaims the real thing.

Marks are considerably easier to explain, for in England each one has a reason and results from a law passed at a given date. This makes it possible for the beginner with an average memory to date a piece at a glance within certain broad limits, even before he has mastered the stylistic changes. Very few, beyond dealers who do it every day, can read date letters precisely without recourse to a book, and with certain well-known exceptions the same applies to the maker's mark, which need not worry us unduly.

In America maker's marks are of much greater importance, for when stamped they are obliged to tell the whole story. As a rule the earlier craftsmen stamped their initials, while those that came later spelt out the full name. Within this formula it is known that some makers changed their mark at a given period in their careers, incorporating a device, such as a crown, or changing the shape of punch, or the style of lettering. This helps to narrow the margin of date on any piece, together with its style and the growing maturity of the craftsman's work.

The first mark stamped in England was the leopard's head, punched in London to show that the piece of plate had been duly tested by assay and proved to be of sterling standard. Pure silver is too soft to manipulate so copper, the only base metal that does not make it too brittle, is used to harden it. The sterling standard in England was 92·5% pure silver. The earliest American silver was largely melted down from old English or Dutch pieces, and so was also of this standard, but between 1792 and 1837 the standard became 89·2% and after 1837 the standard generally used was 90% pure silver.

In 1327 the leopard's head was first stamped and until 1478 it wore no crown. Changes in its expression through the years concern the expert only, but the beginner may pick up a piece in a friend's home and say, 'George IV . . . or later I'd say,' because the creature again lost its crown in 1821. If it wears a crown then the piece was made before 1821.

The maker's mark became law in 1363 and was usually, but not always, a device or a rebus on his name until the mid-seventeenth century, when initials became normal in London. Penalties for any infringements of the law were extremely harsh and the maker's mark was intended as an identification, so that a culprit who used a lower standard would be known. The date letter, probably introduced in about 1478 when the leopard's head became crowned, had much the same purpose, because the warden concerned with the assay might have been bribed to pass substandard silver. The wardens were changed yearly in May and the date letter, intended to identify him, covered each tenure of office and then changed, the B of 1797–8, for instance, becoming C in May. This explains the ascription of date to two years, most of which belongs to the first year, which is the year intended when a single date is given. Every twenty years the style of letter and its shield also changed, so that the first thing, when looking up a date, is to find the right cycle. This system has been very much to our advantage, but forged marks do exist, either transposed or cast from a genuine article, or struck with false punches. It pays to be aware of this possibility, but as it is not only an offence to sell such work but even to have it on the premises, silver bought from a reputable dealer should be safe.

The lion passant became the fourth compulsory mark in 1545, as an indication of invariable standard at a time when King Henry VIII was playing merry havoc with the currency. The inflation he started spiralled through the years, and because coin and plate were freely interchangeable, drastic measures to curb it were taken in 1697. The Britannia Act resulted, when the marking of silver outside London became illegal. Up to this time silver had been marked in dozens of places, some of them officially, and their marks make a *focal* point in many collections of English spoons. Such silver was, in most cases, carefully controlled by a local guild and its marks, if illegal, are in no way fraudulent. For most of these marks a book must be consulted, but early spoons made in Exeter, stamped with a variable punch that always includes a large X, are most frequently found.

The Britannia Act raised the standard for plate to 95·8% pure silver, a softer metal with a glorious glow

that was less suitable for decoration, a fact responsible for the unadorned quality of English Queen Anne silver. This silver was marked with a totally different set of punches, large in themselves, biting into the soft metal and very clear to see. The figure of a seated lady known as Britannia, holding out an olive branch in one hand, a stave in the other, replaced the leopard's head crowned. It is possible to confuse her with 'Hibernia', a Dublin lady similarly seated on silver stamped there after 1730, but the marks accompanying her will always include a crowned harp, distinctively Irish. The Britannia standard was never used in Scotland or Ireland. In England the lion's head erased replaced the lion passant; the maker's mark now consisted of the first two letters of his surname, an impossible situation saved by the ingenuity of men who produced them in great variety, making them distinguishable, although so many began with the same two letters. The Britannia Act was repealed in 1719, the sterling standard and its marks being restored *at the option of the maker*. This is important. Higher standard silver only was used between 1697 and 1719. It has never been forbidden

RIGHT *some British silver marks:*

1 Leopard's head crowned	1689–90 William and Mary
2 Leopard's head crowned	1719–20 George I
3 Leopard's head crowned	1837–38 Victoria
4 Lion passant	1678–79 Charles II
5 Lion passant	1773–74 George III
6 Lion's head erased	1699–1700 William and Mary
7 Britannia	1699–1700
8 Lion rampant	1897–98 Victoria
9 Town mark, crowned 'X' (early Exeter)	1635–38 Charles I
10 Town mark, castle (Exeter) after 1701	1701–02 Anne
11 Town mark, castle (Exeter)	1702–03
12 Town mark, three castles (Newcastle) after 1701	1714–15 Anne
13 Town mark, three castles (Newcastle)	1727–1800
14 Town mark, (York) after 1701	1837–38 Victoria
15 Town mark, three demi lions and one wheatsheaf (Chester)	1701–02 Anne
16 Town mark, three wheatsheaves (Chester) after 1784	1818–19 George IV
17 Town mark, anchor (Birmingham)	1773–74
18, 19, 20 Town mark, crown (Sheffield), 1773–74, 1786–87	1792–93 George III
21, 22 Town marks, castle, thistle, (Edinburgh)	1780–81
23, 24 Town marks, castle, thistle, (Edinburgh)	1820–21 George IV
25, 26 Town mark, tree, fish and bell (Glasgow)	1819–21 William IV
27 Town mark, harp crowned (Dublin)	1747 George II
28 Hibernia (Dublin)	1747

29–33 Complete set of London marks 1678–79 including makers mark.
34–38 Complete set of Newcastle marks 1702–03 taken from a tankard, Blackgate Museum, maker John Ramsay.
39–43 Complete set of Birmingham marks 1798–99 taken from a nutmeg box, makers Willmore & Alston.
44–49 Complete set of Chester marks, 1797–98, taken from a large skewer, maker George Lowe.

and has been used when preferred ever since. In 1700 it became legal once more for certain provincial towns to mark silver and of these Exeter, Newcastle (which started one year later) and Chester are the most likely to be seen. Their marks, as illustrated, were used in addition to the four Britannia standard marks punched in London (or the sterling standard after 1719) making five in all in the provinces. York, one of the finest and oldest guilds, closed down early in the eighteenth century until about 1780, but from then until the office closed in 1858 York work again appears for sale.

The goldsmiths of Birmingham, who stamped their work with an anchor, and those of Sheffield, who used a crown as town mark were granted the right to assay silver in 1773. The use of machinery brought the prices right down to cater for the needs of a new class who now wished to display fine silver in their homes without paying top prices. These two marks, particularly the anchor, are of great importance to the collector with limited space or means, for the Birmingham craftsmen produced an immense range of small objects of excellent quality. Some of these may not be marked, since many of the tiny objects made in Birmingham and other places were exempted from the assay laws during the eighteenth century The list included anything filigree, lockets, and several types of small case, the silver sockets and the bells for a child's coral and whistle, made all over the world from earliest times, and the smallest type of nutmeg grater, which after 1690 when pockets were invented men carried with them to use as required. All these graters were basically in three parts, a body to hold the nut with the grating surface above it, and a hinged lid at either end. They are most collectable. It would also be possible to collect several thousand silver buttons, each one different. Of these the smallest, such as sleeve buttons, or thin, hollow ones, were exempted from assay laws, but of those that were marked the majority were made in Birmingham. Specialization is desirable in such a vast field, and is quite simple with the endless variety of buttons for hunts, regiments, societies and other things; those in America being even wider in scope than the English. American peace medals, so fascinating for their background stories, also make an outstanding subject for a collection in a small space.

But we were talking of marks and it is important to remember, when looking up those accompanying a provincial town mark, that each guild had its own date cycle. The exact style of letter and shape of shield may be found in the London tables, but if a provincial town mark is present, the date must be sought under that heading only. The mark of the sovereign's head was added to the others in 1784, when a tax of sixpence an ounce was imposed. This made five marks in London and six in the provinces and gives another easy method of checking for the beginner.

If the sovereign's head is shown, and the leopard's head is crowned, then the piece was made *between 1784 and 1821*.

The tax of 1784 was dropped in 1890, when the sovereign's head disappeared, so that four marks only (five in the provinces), with an *uncrowned* leopard's head, means that the piece was stamped after 1890. These marks are the backbone of the English hall-marking system. The many variations are technicalities that do not concern the average collector.

Silver was also produced in a great number of places in Scotland, though Edinburgh was the most important. There the system was somewhat different, for the assay master's initials were punched on the right, in addition to those of the maker, on the left, with the Edinburgh mark of a triple towered castle in between and, after 1681, the date letter. Before this came in, there were only three marks, but be careful to check all other indications of age, for marks do tend to fade with rubbing. In 1759 the assay master's mark was replaced by a thistle, another of those milestones that enable the beginner to make a spot assessment. The sovereign's head duty stamp was also imposed in Scotland, and punched on plate assayed in Edinburgh or Glasgow from 1784.

Therefore the thistle mark, with a triple towered castle but no sovereign's head, must mean that the piece was made in Edinburgh between 1759 and 1784.

The silver made in other parts of Scotland was not officially sanctioned and so they dispensed with the more tiresome aspects of law, including this duty and its mark. One should not infer, however, that such work was inferior. That of Aberdeen, Inverness and Perth, in particular, was of high quality. Glasgow's hallmarking system was sporadic until 1819. The town mark of a tree, fish and bell, in variable form, was stamped between the maker's initials which were punched twice, and occasionally a date letter was added, mostly an 'S' in various forms during the eighteenth century. In 1819 Glasgow opened an official and regular assay office punching a lion rampant as standard mark after the tree, or date letter, the sovereign's head and maker's mark. From 1890 when the king's head disappeared to 1914 when a thistle took its place there were only four marks, an

RIGHT *The Howard Grace cup, ivory mounted silver-gilt, English 1525–6*

easy dating device. Five, including the lion rampant and thistle, signifies Glasgow between 1914 and 1964 when the office closed.

One of the greatest misconceptions regarding silver is that if the word 'sterling' is stamped, the piece must be American. In fact this word was used on English and Irish silver in at least a dozen ways, most of them early, while it was not adopted in America until 1865. If the silver found for sale is old, it is most likely to have been made in Cork or Limerick as both cities adopted this stamp in 1710, while later work is probably American, though it need not be. The marks stamped by Baltimore between 1814 and 1830 are unlikely to affect the small collector of American work who must rely on the story initials have to tell. These have led to a totally different approach to research into silver, focusing on family history which itself becomes a dating device. The first American silver was made in Boston in 1634 and shortage of metal, particularly in those early times, meant that silver was largely ordered for important family occasions, such as a marriage or christening. This was commemorated by the engraving of the relevant initials and, because the event was recorded, research can date it exactly. A great American favourite was the porringer, a round, usually bulbous bowl, with one flat, pierced handle on which the initials appeared. The piercing was highly individualistic to start with, and in New York was so intricate that there was scarcely room for the initials, but by the mid-eighteenth century piercing had become largely keyhole, and consequently less interesting. Inscriptions and armorials engraved on larger pieces, as in England, also help to date silver exactly, for they sometimes have the arms of one family entwined with those of another, signifying a marriage, but this, of course, stopped after the War for Independence (1775–81).

ABOVE *an American silver porringer by Benjamin Burt, Boston, c 1760*

BELOW *a covered, inverted pear-shaped sugar bowl; Philadelphia c 1780*

STYLES IN THEIR PERIODS

STYLES sometimes had the same names at different periods in England and America, but where the names are totally different the English has been used.

England	America
William and Mary 1689–1702	1685–1720
Queen Anne (with early Georgian) 1700–27	1720–50
Mid-Georgian 1728–70	(Chippendale) 1750–85
Neo-Classic (or Adam) 1760–1800	1783–1815
Regency 1800–30	1815–40 (Empire)
Victorian 1830–1900	c. 1840–1900
Art Nouveau c. 1870–1920	c. 1875–1920

Silver for the Tea Table

TEAPOTS AND KETTLES · TEA SETS · CREAM JUGS · SUGAR BOWLS
ENGLISH PORRINGERS · SPOON TRAYS · SUGAR TONGS · GRAPE SCISSORS · TEA STRAINERS
STRAINER SPOONS · TEA CADDIES · CADDY SPOONS

Tea drinking in eighteenth-century England was an elegant ritual requiring a great array of fine silver from the most sumptuous teapots and bottles to the tiniest caddy spoons. All these objects were also made in America, and all are collected avidly today.

Queen Anne silver is beyond the reach of the small collector, but an understanding of its features is important as nothing illustrates so well the meaning of the elusive word 'quality'. Queen Anne's reign (1702–14) was totally within the Britannia period and the soft metal of the standard then in force naturally created the style of this period, which is distinguished by the combination of thick silver, fine workmanship and beautiful, unfussy lines. Decoration, if present, was largely confined to applied mouldings or cut-card-work, which consisted of foliage or geometric patterns cut from sheet silver and soldered on to the flat surface. This gave strength artistically around joints of handles or spouts, and sometimes also radiated from the finial on a lid. It was less often used in America, but is not unknown.

The Queen Anne teapot was pear-shaped, very often octagonal in England, but only rarely so in America, with or without a moulded band applied around the centre. The kettle mirrored the style of the pot, although the earliest examples sat down rather more squatly than the pots, which curved in to a circular base. Fewer kettles were made in America but those that were also have this wide, flat bottom and mostly appear without the burner and stand, which were exciting features of these lovely objects.

Armorials were almost invariably engraved on the plain surfaces of Queen Anne silver, the cartouches (surroundings) being handled in a vigorous, almost architectural style. The value of a piece is sadly reduced if this engraving has been erased or altered in any way, as it destroys uniformity in the patina. This, of course, applies to the removal of arms or inscriptions on silver of any period, wherever it was made, and is a point to watch. The lovely line of the Queen Anne style has been reproduced from the nineteenth century onwards, and is more pleasant to live with than many other period pieces. Nevertheless the heavily decorated styles that came later are very popular, particularly in America and a good test for quality is to try to visualize the basic form, measuring the unadorned object for balance before looking at it again as it really is.

While the pear-shaped form died out in England after 1720 it continued to be made occasionally in America for a considerable time to come in addition to the bullet- or globular-shaped pot, and the inverted-pear-shape, at which Boston craftsmen excelled. The bullet form (1715–45) was occasionally octagonal to begin with in England, with a straight spout, flat hinged lid fitting flush, a little engraving around the shoulders above the armorials, and a circular slightly stepped base. In Scotland, where workmanship was excellent, the globe was totally round, balanced on a short stem above the foot, and instantly recognizable. Over the years American silversmiths, particularly the enterprising craftsmen of New York, made a feature of the spout which could be beaded, fluted, faceted or richly ornamented, often with applied decoration below and finished with a realistic duck neck that was often quite elaborate.

LEFT *a George II bullet-shaped teapot, London; 1738*

RIGHT *a collection of Irish silver: Helmet cream jug, c 1735; coffee pot chased with hunting scenes by Joseph Jackson, Dublin c 1780; oval teapot and stand with bright cut engraving by Richard Sawyer, Dublin 1806; dish ring, c 1785*

BELOW *a collection of Scottish silver: Teapot by David Mitchell, Edinburgh, 1739; bowl by Lothian and Robertson, Edinburgh 1753; cream jug by William Ayton, 1746*

ABOVE *a detail of the top of a teapot by Samuel Casey*
BELOW *American c 1760, showing interlaced strapwork*

TOP RIGHT *silver by Hester Bateman:*
a sweetmeat basket, 1790; an oval teapot 1781; mustard
pot, 1783; oval teapot, 1783

FAR RIGHT *a cream jug dated c 1750–60*

The finest English craftsmen made some superlative inverted-pear-shaped pots following on the bullet-shape, but in America the form was more popular and the average example was superior. They had engraved or embossed decoration tumbling over the shoulders, and below it was engraved a coat-of-arms or a crest . . . or both, one on each side. Embossing, incidentally, is a technique that removes no silver but, pushing it out from behind, creates a raised pattern. 'Repoussé' is the same thing except that the embossing has been touched up from the front, giving it extra definition. A particularly pleasing example of the inverted-pear-shaped teapot by Benjamin Burt (*c.* 1760–65), has embossed flowers and scroll decoration standing out over the shoulders like lace. Lids were slightly domed and finials varied but a somewhat taller version of pots of this shape may be found from the middle of the century, plastered all over with decoration. If the teapot is genuine rococo, flowers, scrolls and decoration will stand out from a plain surface. The Victorians, attempting the same thing in the nineteenth century, confused the eye with a matted ground. They also liked to 'improve' any plain surface by adding grandiose ornamentation to old silver, thus ruining the piece.

The Industrial Revolution brought machine assistance to English goldsmiths in about 1770, which changed the style and texture of all articles. The silver was rolled very thinly, so that the cylindrical forms of pot such as the drum, oval flat top and boat shape that followed, could be made (and sold today) at a fraction of the previous price. These were decorated, particularly in the last decade, in bright cut engraving, a technique that polished as it cut, giving a jewelled appearance. America was suffering turbulent times and goldsmiths had little work until about 1790, when the War for Independence was over, but then they too used the swags, garlands and other light, symmetrical patterns that were perfectly balanced and created the neo-classic style of decoration.

Within these basic forms variations occurred, such as the wide flutes used in Boston, and the high domes that occasionally transformed the shape, whether oval or drum. New York goldsmiths favoured a band of bright cut engravings above and below the draped ornament, occasionally finishing with beaded rims. Also known in Boston, these rims were nevertheless unmistakably a feature of Philadelphia where the beads were small, tightly strung, and usually the only decoration (unless more was added later), in the

ABOVE *silver-giltcovered cup, London, 1700*   BELOW *a highly ornate teapot c 1845*   RIGHT *18th century kettle; American, c 1720*

PREVIOUS PAGE *a four piece teaset by Paul Storr, 1815. This was about mid-period and quite plain compared to his later, ornate work*

LEFT *two sauce boats, London; 1740–41. The handles are of the flying scrolled, leaf-capped type*

RIGHT *an American cream jug by Benjamin Burt, c 1750*

BELOW *two 18th century cream jugs, the one on the right is by William Hughes, Dublin; c 1750. Notice the typical Irish features – the moulded rib, the lion masks and paw and shell feet (page 32)*

ABOVE *a covered sugar bowl by John McFee, Philadelphia;* *c 1790. The pierced gallery and narrow beaded borders are* *typical of Philadelphian work*

TOP RIGHT *oval tea and coffee set, decorated all over with* *the Greek key pattern; the tea and coffee pots have ebony* *handles. London, 1802*

BELOW RIGHT *a sugar box by Daniel Greenough;* *American, c 1715*

manner often used by Hester Bateman in London.

Careful examination for damage or flaws is particularly important with this thin rolled silver. Look for worn patches, even holes, which also occur in heavily embossed work when the craftsman has hammered too hard; see that the hinge works correctly and that the lid, easily bent, fits tightly; and see that there are no repairs around handle or spout sockets, or extra solder where it should not be. In England, every part of a piece of silver that can be detached should be hallmarked separately, although quite often the maker's mark and lion passant will suffice on the lid.

From the turn of the century teapots were usually made as a part of a matching set, comprising cream jug, sugar basin, a coffee pot and sometimes a tray. In the early classical years, these *could* be beautifully made in clear line, but as the rococo revival (1830–60), Renaissance revival (1860–80) and a plethora of other bygone styles suggested themselves to craftsmen with insufficient education, the objects could take almost any form, while decoration varied between restrained good taste (occasionally) and an over-exuberance which was at times appalling. A show of wealth was more important to many than a proper understanding of style, but anything of quality in the early years had applied ornamentation in a balanced style, often as a classical frieze or as gadroons, which make a lobed edge to a foot, rim, shoulders or any other projecting part; or as flutes, those attractive rounded channels that usually rise, straight or spiralling, from the base of an object. Taste, formed by looking at the best, is difficult to describe, but in nineteenth-century silver the piece that has line and decoration harmoniously balanced will stand out and be well worth buying, if it is also in good condition.

In England the first tea services did not appear until about 1785 but an outstanding example in the New York City Museum, made by Pieter de Riemer (1738–1814) of New York, is dated 1765–75. This has an inverted-pear-shaped pot, chased over the shoulders with delightful rococo flowers, punctuated with scrolls swirling in either direction, standing out from an uncluttered background; a covered sugar basin and a pear-shaped jug, mounted on a circular base with a short spool stem. All are decorated in the same way, chasing being a technique that indents, from front or back, without removing any metal (ranging from embossing at its strongest, to flat chasing). There is a type of close gadrooning on the inside of the rim of the basin that is peculiar to New York goldsmiths.

The 'pitcher' type cream jug is a form seen less often than the three-legged variety that preceded it, but it was in vogue from about 1765 to 1780, and decoration

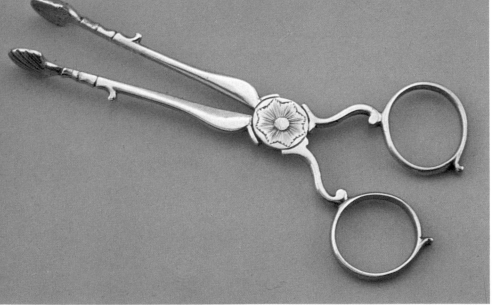

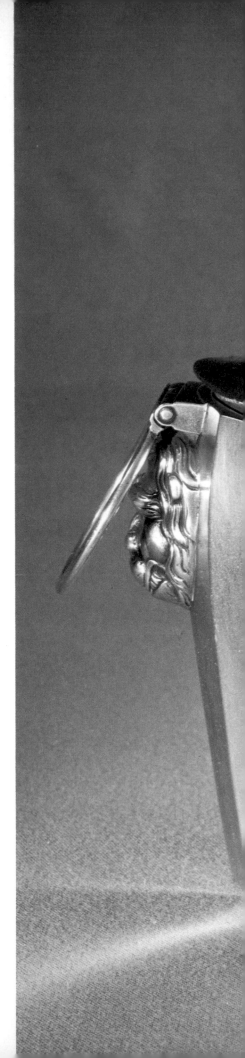

TOP *an American sugar box by Edward Winslow (1699–1753)*
who was a grandson of one of the Pilgrim Fathers

ABOVE *a pair of unmarked 18th century American sugar tongs*
RIGHT *a tea caddy by James Black, Philadelphia; c 1800*

ABOVE *a five piece tea set by S Kirk and Son, Baltimore, 1903–24; ornate work repoussé and chased with Italianate scenes and classical ruins*

RIGHT *a tea kettle on lampstand, New York; c 1840. This is copied from a George II original*

took the form of stamped ornament, gadrooning or beading around the foot.

Originally tea was taken without cream, and the first jugs are very rare. They were covered from *c.* 1705, and after about 1720 they were rather like a mug set on a round foot with a small applied lip. The three-legged jug, however, with a bulbous body, wavy rim and double-scroll handle (1735–70) was much more popular. Made prolifically they are within the means of the average, if not the small collector, plain jugs being considerably more expensive than those with embossed decoration. In America, where the three cabriole legs were usually shell topped, their line was less elegant (except in Philadelphia), the waist less pronounced, and their style of decoration, while most attractive and varied, totally different.

There is no mistaking the American version, but the Irish also made these jugs quite superlatively and though the practised eye can pick them out immediately, it is hard to pinpoint the differences. The Irish jugs were slightly larger, with a more pronounced lip, and usually, though not invariably, had

a moulded rib around the centre. This moulded centre rib also appeared on some English jugs. Some were chased all over, those from Ireland in the most imaginative way with buds, flowers, milkmaids or other pastoral scenes, while the English were generally more conventional. The best of these jugs were made in thick silver, with particularly thick rims. A prospective buyer should make sure that any embossing is original for it could have been added later. The three feet could be paws with lion masks above, ball and claw or shell. While there is no rule, a plain jug with a wide lip, well-moulded mid-rib and lion's mask and paw feet is probably Irish. This should, of course, bear Irish marks, but makers were careless and often forgot!

The last quarter of the century saw the tall, elegant helmet-shaped jug with a slender stem and round base sometimes set on a square plinth. These were also well made in Ireland and usually lightly engraved in a pretty neo-classic style but the silver was machine rolled, and can be very thin and easily damaged, while the high sloping handle is very

33

fragile. The 'coal scuttle' type of flat-bottomed jug that followed, 1790–1810, was also lightly engraved, but both the metal itself and the shape, which was rather taller in America, was more robust. Less elegant and certainly less popular, these are considerably cheaper and often present better value to the collector. From this style evolved the boat-shape, seen in many forms during the nineteenth century.

Sugar bowls were a luxury at first, and the majority of those who could afford to drink tea may have made do with any old thing, such as a porringer (or caudle cup), those multi-purpose seventeenth-century bulbous bowls that had two caryatid handles (cast with draped females as thumb grips), strong naturalistic embossing and a rounded cover which could be used upside down as a separate dish when its top decoration was of the platform type. These came in all sizes, their style changing in the Britannia period, but the small ones were often used as tea cups before china cups came in. These bowls were also made by America's finest makers, such as John Coney (1656–1722), usually without the embossing or cover. Those glorious New York low bowls, circular on a small moulded foot, with caryatid handles and six simulated panels containing embossed or engraved decoration, would look even better on the table.

The first bowls made for sugar, *c.* 1720, were plain and round, like a miniature punch bowl, with a rounded cover surmounted by a plain rim, intended to reverse and use as a tray for spoons after stirring for there were no saucers. Spoon trays are considered collectable items today and were often made after they were no longer needed, as was the stand for a teapot from which it had become separated. The covered sugar bowls were slightly taller in America and changed their shape through the years, growing in height and taking a domed cover with a finial before giving way to the sugar basket in England, in about 1765. Originally, even these baskets could be vase-shaped, often pierced in the classical manner, with festoons of drapery, stylized leaves and flowers (particularly in the honeysuckle motif), scrolls, shells and so forth, with the blue glass liner showing through. These baskets had swing handles and often a shaped rim, but the vase-shape spread sideways very quickly, soon becoming boat-shaped, decorated in any classic revival form and usually because the silver was thin, with bright cut engraving. At the same time bowls for sugar continued to be made in Ireland, three-legged like the cream jugs, with shell, lion's mask and paw, or sometimes even a human mask at the joint. Fairly shallow, they were the most graceful of things, with a widely everted rim, usually scalloped and with deeply indented lines curving horizontally around them. Such bowls were often made in Cork or Limerick, later ones being embossed and not nearly as distinctive.

Sugar baskets were never as popular in America, but they were made between 1795 and 1820, with swing handles, or occasionally with two tall loop handles, curving out gracefully from the base. Nevertheless, the sugar urn was one of the most distinctive of American forms, without English parallel. Tall and elegant it epitomizes all that is graceful in the neoclassic form. It was usually decorated with bright cut engraving in a light, restrained manner, or with applied masks or other heavy motifs, which however correct for the period, are much less dainty. The form, basically a goblet on a round foot, usually set on a square base, has a tall, slender baluster cover, usually with an urn finial, the whole presenting reversing curves in the most balanced form.

RIGHT *a tea urn by S Kirk and Son, Baltimore, c 1850. Its height is 18 inches*

BELOW *a cream jug by John Pollock with hoof-feet and a spool neck; 1739*

ABOVE *an American tea strainer; c 1780*

RIGHT *a caddy spoon made by Cocks and Bettridge, Birmingham, 1811. The mark on the back shows firstly the maker's stamp and then the king's head, the lion passant, the anchor of Birmingham and the date letter*

New York craftsmen sometimes used a domed cover instead of the tall spool, giving a totally different and less attractive appearance, despite excellent quality in workmanship. Those made in Philadelphia, however, can be picked out anywhere for their distinctive beaded rims and the pierced gallery that surrounds the rim of the bowl. The earliest tea services sometimes contained such a sugar urn, but as time went on styles became increasingly similar to those in England.

Elegant manners, of course, would not allow fingers dipping into sugar containers, and sugar tongs were made from the beginning of the eighteenth century, the earliest ones being modelled on the andirons used for the fire. These were followed by the scissor type (1725–60), often with leaves entwined around the shell grips, flowers, or other motifs. Marks are important on these for they were frequently copied during the nineteenth century and the originals are hard to find; particularly those in the form of a stork, the hinge pin forming his eye, the best of which are found to be carrying a baby when opened. Tongs created by an ever-varying series of scrolls and twists are more usual. Shell grips are the rule and compared with the grape scissors of Victorian times they are more like the scissors used for embroidery, while grape scissors more nearly resembled the cutting out type of scissors. Nevertheless both show sufficient variety to be most collectable.

Cast tongs, more brittle and easily damaged, particularly at the weak top, came in around 1770. They were often made in five parts, grips, side pieces and connecting bend, all of which are so varied that it is hard to find any two identical. Prices are most reasonable, going even lower for the plain bow type (1780 1820) made in a single strip of silver, yet they appear to be a rather neglected subject, particularly in America. By this time (after 1784) shortage of silver was no longer a problem in the States, for discarded English coins created a good supply. This metal, only 90% pure silver, is described there as 'coin' silver, differentiating it from sterling (92·5%). Tongs made of this standard would not stand up too well to wear, but they are comparable in price with many twentieth-century gimmicks in silver and they *are* antique. The bow type can be infinitely varied, basic outline taking any form known to table silver, such as hourglass or fiddle pattern, often with a few extras for originality. Grips, mostly oblong and rather pointed, were often engraved in keeping with the main pattern, frequently bright cut, although a simple edging device may be all that is used. All English sugar tongs should be hall-marked with at least two stamps, and they will drop in value if repairs have damaged these marks.

Tea strainers did not come in before 1790 when they showed considerable variety in both piercing and handles. Strainers pre-dating this were usually considerably larger, having been intended for making punch. These will look attractive in any collection, and so will strainer spoons, probably used by early tea drinkers to remove floating leaves, in the same way that they have been used to skim foreign bodies from communion wine ever since the middle ages. These spoons, daintily pierced, had a long thin stem with a small pointed end.

Tea was imported into England in chests and sold loose, so that a container for the precious leaves was necessary. The result was the tea caddy, called a cannister until about 1790 and the American version was not noticeably different. The earliest caddies arrived with Queen Anne, and were gloriously plain with well-engraved arms, rectangular or octagonal in shape, with a little dome centrally on top, but they were not very practical and plain boxes with a hinged lid covering the whole top took their place in about 1715. These are more easily managed and are infinitely more popular with collectors who use them in many ways about the house. They were made until 1750, variations in form being minor and decoration changing with the times. It is most unusual to find a plain

caddy after the sterling standard was restored and the finest craftsmen, particularly the Huguenots, found them a wonderful medium for pure rococo. During the last part of this period vase-shaped caddies were also made, often with a small round top and almost always decorated in the rococo style. Because they cannot be put to practical use they are among the least expensive objects of comparable workmanship, but the decoration must be original.

Tea was outlandishly expensive, resulting in theft, so that after about 1740 caddies were kept in a beautiful box that could be locked, made of varying materials, sometimes silver mounted, and usually lined with shagreen. Rich people always had at least two caddies, often made in pairs, for skill in blending tea at table was of high snob value, but these boxes were made to hold three, one slightly larger, for the sugar which was also worth stealing. It is a collector's dream to find a full set in its original box. After 1760 the caddy itself was fitted with a lock, and the *bombé* form was probably the last that lacked it.

The oval caddy with a flush fitting cover, domed from 1790, and with a variety of finials, is probably the best known to collectors, for this type of caddy was made in quantity, is light and attractive and useful today. The thin rolled silver could only be

ABOVE *a set of three vase-shaped caddies by Samuel Taylor; London, 1749. The larger one is for sugar. The case is of fish skin and is velvet lined*

ABOVE RIGHT *a set of rectangular tea caddies and sugar box with box with their veneered ebony case, by Abraham Buteaux, English; 1730*

engraved, but the symmetrical curves of this pretty style suited it particularly well. At the same time, however, caddies were made in other classical forms, thicker in metal, heavily embossed and applied with the more sturdy motifs of the times, while another type copied the original chests exactly, even down to Chinese characters engraved on the front. These are searched out avidly by keen collectors.

Large sea shells were packed in the original chests when the tea was dispatched from China, and these were used to scoop out the tea in suitable quantities for sale. Naturally the finest caddy spoons, *c.* 1770, were based on this motif, kept in the caddy itself and used for measuring tea into the pot. The earliest of these spoons were made in Sheffield and had a very short handle, but during the last decade of the eighteenth century the handle lengthened a little and became more variable in shape. Shell spoons were always popular and continued to be made until about 1830, particularly in London where those by Hester

Bateman were quite distinctive with an attractively flared rim, and bright cut handle.

Caddy spoons of all sorts continued to be made until after 1850, and throughout this time they took every conceivable plain form, the bowls round, square, oval, heart- or acorn-shaped, the handles taking any pattern in keeping with the date, such as hourglass after 1815 or fiddle and thread from 1810 to 1830. These were particularly easy to fake, by marrying up a cut-down tea or salt spoon handle, complete with a good set of marks, to any old bowl. This type of handle sometimes also appears with other shaped bowls, including the shovel, which may be decorated in endless ways, pierced (rare), engraved and embossed, in any combination imaginable. Similar spoons with a long handle are also sold as caddy spoons, but were probably made for sugar or jam. They are just one good reason why these little objects should be bought from a specialist dealer. Although they are small and comparatively inexpensive it is

BELOW *a tea caddy by John Farnell; English, 1723. It was probably engraved later, c 1745*

still fatally easy to make mistakes, for the marking, construction and method of decoration are all variable and faking is particularly easy.

So far we have said nothing about the 'exotics' of this field – the eagle's wing, the hand, the jockey cap, the mussel shell, the fish, or the leaf in many forms – but nearly all articles and books on this specialist subject deal with them almost exclusively. Such spoons had very little connection with the tea table, being fanciful gimmicks. They were mostly made by the famous craftsmen of Birmingham who were such masters of the diecast method. Among the greatest were Joseph Taylor, specialist in the jockey cap, Joseph Willmore, Cocks and Bettridge and Samuel Pemberton, who all worked in the early 19th century.

Some of these spoons were also made in London, notably those with the hand and the mussel shell, but on the whole the capital was concerned with quality and their spoons are thicker in metal than those made in Birmingham, which can be very thin.

A six piece American tea and coffee set with matching hot water kettle on lampstand, by Thomas Fletcher, Philadelphia; c 1840. The embossing is of very high quality

Dinner Table Silver

SALTS · EWERS AND BASINS · FORKS · MUSTARD POTS · PEPPER POTS
CASTORS · BRAZIERS and CHAFING DISHES · IRISH DISH RINGS · SOUP TUREENS
SAUCE TUREENS · SAUCE LADLES · SUGAR SIFTERS · SOUP LADLES · SAUCE BOATS
PAP BOATS · GORGETS · ENTREE DISHES · DINNER SERVICES · PLATTERS · PLATES · SKEWERS
MARROW SCOOPS · CHEESE SCOOPS · KNIFE RESTS · SERVING SPOONS · BASTING SPOONS
MAZARINS · FISH SLICES · CAKE BASKETS · BELLS

The great Salts of the Middle Ages are among the most impressive pieces to be seen in a museum collection today, but only those lucky enough to attend a Livery or College dinner in England are likely to see them in use. Whatever form they took, they stood like a centrepiece on the High Table, the host and more important guests sitting round and dipping their meat into the tiny salt container somewhere near the top of the structure. The salt was of enormous social importance and, in a different way, so also were the ewers and basins – to be seen only in great collections now. Sometimes massive and always marvellous they illustrate a different standard of table manners, rather than a lack of them, for forks were not used until after 1660 and fingers tended to become messy when diners picked up their food, dipped it into the salt (those further down the table had smaller salts standing beside their own trencher, or wooden plate) and ate it. Warm scented water was therefore brought into the Dining Hall in a ewer, poured into the richly embossed basin, and passed among the diners, who washed several times during a meal.

Some salts, however, were not so grand, such as the lovely Elizabethan bell type, which with its gracious curves was a purely English form with no Continental influences, or those with three or sometimes four arms reaching up on which a plate could be stood, protecting the precious grains from dust. One of the earliest salts in New England, superbly well made c. 1700 by John Allen (1671–1760) and John Edwards (1671–1746) followed this style. It stands nearly six inches high, with two bands of bold, spiral gadroons above and below the double spool stem. This has a lovely octagonal base and top from which four scrolled arms arise, surrounding the circular indent for salt.

Gadroons also featured on late-seventeenth-century trencher salts, but the plain octagonal form made until 1740, is more typical of the unadorned simplicity found with the Queen Anne style. To start with, they were round and beaten up from a single sheet of silver, as were many of the octagonal examples, the skirt and shoulders beautifully incurved, although these were often cast in two parts. Quite a few made in Boston survived, but the earliest, a lovely octagonal trencher, was made in New York and commemorates a 1691 wedding. Another type, round and beautifully decorated standing on a pedestal base, was also made after 1725, but these are rare. The word 'salt-cellar' incidentally, is repetitive, the second word having derived from the French 'sel' meaning salt.

After the small round three-legged salts came in, c. 1735, collecting becomes simplified, for these were made in quantity in both England and America. Quality is another matter. Salt, the corroding enemy of silver, has worn through any that have not been well cared for, as glass liners were used only for

LEFT *a pair of George II scallop shell-shaped butter dishes by Paul de Lamerie, 1742*

43

pierced examples. Gilding the interior was not done before 1740. All salts have suffered and the collector's job is to find examples that have done so less than others. If the marks are clearly stamped he can then think about refinements such as lion mask and paw feet, gadrooned borders, and good line. It is surprising just how varied these little objects can be, and how much decoration could be crammed on to the available space during the nineteenth century.

Pierced salts, usually oval, with a blue glass liner, and with four dainty feet, appeared in about 1760, when mustard pots also became fashionable. These were often pierced in the same way and early examples had graceful scrolling, sometimes a wavy rim, and later geometric patterns or bar piercing overlaid with applied neo-classic motifs. Other shapes came and went, but salts of this basic type never really ceased to be made, unpierced with a bead or thread edge, engraved, sometimes in combination with limited piercing, or with applied decoration, with the feet made of stamped-out strips of metal. Mustard pots followed the line of salts without giving the same appearance, as the handle (usually scroll), the domed lid (only rarely flat) and the thumbpiece (as varied as those on tankards) totally change the outline.

Towards the end of the century, when decoration, if used, was very restrained, boat-shaped salts, with loop handles, were made like a miniature sweetmeat basket, followed, for a short period, by a rather heavy oblong type, on four bun feet, often with a gadrooned rim. From then on salts usually revived old forms, a great number like other table silver, being made in Chester or Birmingham.

Pepper pots, with the exception of those made for kitchen use (cylindrical and low domed similar to the muffineer used for sprinkling spices on to muffins), generally followed the style of sugar castors, on a miniature scale. These first appeared towards the end of the seventeenth century in the cylindrical or 'lighthouse' form. They had a round, domed, pierced cover, which with its finial accounted for more than half of the total height of seven to eight inches, often with gadroons below it and around the base, and the body plain or engraved with armorials only. It was important that the cover should fit tightly. This, sometimes merely punched with holes, could be given an added richness by interesting piercing or the addition of an engraved pattern embodying the piercing in an integrated whole. Bartholomew le Roux, a Huguenot working in New York, 1689–1713, made a superb example soon after 1700.

Castors during the eighteenth century were almost invariably made in sets of three, the tallest for sugar, the other two for spices, pepper or mustard, which was at that time served dry and kept in a blind castor, the piercing only simulated. The Queen Anne period brought in the pear-shaped castor, more often round until 1715 and after 1730 (octagonal in the intervening period) in heavy silver of superb quality. Piercing was mostly geometric with engraved armorials as the only decoration, while applied mouldings around the centre, like the foot and finial, were cast, the body being hand-raised. As time went on this shape became even more sharply concave above the moulding, like a slim-waisted ballet dancer pirouetting. The quality of the piercing, no longer necessarily geometric, makes the difference between a good or superlative example, but overall workmanship, particularly fit,

LEFT *a salt cellar by Paul de Lamerie, with grotesque iron masks, gadroon rim and three paw supports; 1740*

TOP RIGHT *a pair of trencher salts set on beaded rims with lobed and fluted bodies by Pierre Harache, English; 1694. In the centre is a kitchen pepper by William Hinton, 1713.* CENTRE *is a detail of the mark on the kitchen pepper; the maker's stamp, Britannia, the lion's head erased and the harp of Dublin are visible*

BELOW LEFT *a sauce boat by Paul Revere, Boston; c 1770. The three legs are raised on scroll supports headed and terminated by rococo shell motifs; the double scroll handle is leaf capped, applied at the top with a putto mask and joined to the body by a cinquefoil*

BELOW RIGHT *detail of the putto mask of Paul Revere's sauceboat left. Attractive masks like this are frequently found in the work of American silversmiths*

condition and, in England, clear marks, are all important. From about 1735 the 'bowl' below the moulding took an inverted-pear-shape, making a vase of it, while maintaining the waist above, often heavily embossed in rococo, or later, neo-classic forms, which detracted from the basic elegance but added a new interest when well done. In Boston and (more often) New York, castors generally followed the same lines, although frequently less waisted, as with the tripod cream jugs, and sometimes with refinements of shape all their own. Castors were only rarely made in England after sugar baskets came in (c. 1775) and then were thin, with machine-made parts.

Piercing was always a feature in American workmanship to which braziers (or chafing dishes) lent themselves admirably. Intended for the preparation of sauces at table, or for keeping food hot, these had an openwork body, allowing a draught to fan the hot charcoal they contained. The earliest, made in quantity by John Coney and other Boston goldsmiths were straight-sided, their legs continuing up like a frame, to create three scrolled arms above, on which a plate or dish could be placed. The framework remained basically unchanged, but the whole became more elegant and shapely, the piercing more imaginative and the arms lower and more beautifully scrolled. There was usually a wooden handle fitting into a silver socket attached to the frame, and later, when a spirit burner was incorporated, the pierced sides became purely decorative.

A few of these were also made in England, but the far less imposing dish cross, made from about 1750 to 1850, was more usual and adaptable, for the four feet could be moved to fit a round or oval plate, with the

ABOVE *a tureen by Boulton and Fothergill, Birmingham; 1776*

BELOW *a bowl by Cornelius Kierstede, New York, first quarter 18th century. Kierstede was one of the outstanding Dutch immigrant smiths and this is a particularly fine example of a New York bowl*

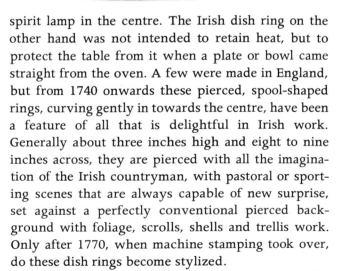

spirit lamp in the centre. The Irish dish ring on the other hand was not intended to retain heat, but to protect the table from it when a plate or bowl came straight from the oven. A few were made in England, but from 1740 onwards these pierced, spool-shaped rings, curving gently in towards the centre, have been a feature of all that is delightful in Irish work. Generally about three inches high and eight to nine inches across, they are pierced with all the imagination of the Irish countryman, with pastoral or sporting scenes that are always capable of new surprise, set against a perfectly conventional pierced background with foliage, scrolls, shells and trellis work. Only after 1770, when machine stamping took over, do these dish rings become stylized.

The great tureens that brought soup or stew to table from about 1730 would not fit on to one of these dish

rings for they were oval in shape on four well-cast feet, in the form of a hoof, shell or scroll, with strongly cast animal masks, sheaves of wheat or foliage above them. Strong is the keyword, for all decoration was cast in high relief and applied, sometimes accentuating its quality by suitable restraint, at others so cramming available space that nothing can be properly seen. At best they are magnificent, well beyond the means of most of us but beware of nineteenth-century copies, when the man of little taste could make terrible mistakes, mixing up his revived styles. During the neo-classic period these tureens had an oval pedestal base, sometimes with their own stands, at first (c 1760–70) decorated with applied revival motifs (never as common in America) and later, when silver had become thin, with shallow hollow fluting, the channels curving gracefully into the silver rather than

47

rounding out. Elegant loop handles complete the delightful shape, but additional decoration beyond light gadrooning or beaded edges is rare and found only in the finest examples.

Sauce tureens, unusual before 1770, were really smaller versions of the same thing, normally made in pairs or layer sets. The ladles for use with them also followed the line of the soup ladle of the period, on a smaller scale, their bowls only occasionally fluted, usually round, and sometimes with fairly steep sides. They make a delightful collection which must include sugar sifters. These are identical except for piercing in the bowl and are excitingly varied, their stems taking every form and style of decoration known to spoons (see Chapter VII) from 1770 onwards.

Soup ladles appeared very much earlier but are not commonly found before the mid-Georgian period, when they often had a beautifully fluted bowl set on a long arched and delicately engraved Old English handle, bent slightly back at the tip. Rat-tails are rarely found on ladles, the joint of stem and bowl more often being made with the less attractive rounded drop, or double drop, surrounded by a plain shield. The slight ridge, however, running down the back of the stem and usual with rat-tail, may be found, particularly when the ladles were made in Ireland where they were generally more delicate, the shell more splayed, and the engraving lighter. On later examples the stem loses its arch, frequently being of fiddle, thread and shell pattern.

Sauceboats, which pre-dated the tureens, were very important silver objects, those before 1730 double lipped and very wide, and astronomically expensive. Few pieces enjoyed more attention from the great craftsmen, or were more extravagantly decorated, particularly in rococo, for their size. They usually

had three or four feet, cast in the usual variety of forms, with the strengthening mask at the joint above, but exceptions occasionally appeared with pedestal bases decorated in a great variety of ways. Handles, which were double scrolled, or leaf-capped flying scrolled on conventional models, became dolphins, serpents or other marine objects on the exotic pieces and quite frequently the whole boat took the form of a shell to which half the undersea world was clinging. Edges too, varied considerably, from a plain wavy rim, gadroons or punched edges to anything imaginable composed of shells, scrolls and similar mouldings. The conventional sauceboat, with all these features uncluttered by extraneous matter is most attractive and varied, those made in Ireland and America more often taking the simple form. Tiny boats, low and rather flat and, incidentally, with no feet or handles, are called pap boats and were intended

BELOW LEFT *a set of three Queen Anne castors by Henry Greene; 1704. Notice the baluster bodies, the bayonet covers and the fine piercing.*
BELOW *a set of three baluster castors by Samuel Wood; 1758*

FOLLOWING PAGES: *left, a standing salt by Jeremiah Dummer, American 1645–1718. right, a fine example of the great salt, English; c 1610*

for feeding infants. It always strikes me that the gorget, a child's silver bib, would be a necessity, for such feeding must have been a messy business. These boats were beautifully decorated with engraved scenes, particularly in Philadelphia.

Although sauce tureens largely replaced the sauce-boat in neo-classic times the boat continued to be made and it is important to study style before buying nineteenth-century examples, particularly with fanciful specimens, for they lent themselves well to misinterpretation. The entrée or vegetable dish made for strong contrast on the table, for these dishes, oval, round, octagonal or cushion-shaped, introduced in about 1760, were severely plain, rarely taking more decoration than engraved arms or gadrooned edges. They were essentially practical, even the handle to the cover being removable so that the cover could be used as an extra dish itself. The handle, often no more than a ring, albeit sometimes a decorated one, could take the form of a family crest to imposing effect, surrounded, on occasion, by strengthening foliage. Because their purpose was to keep food hot these dishes very often sat on a hot water dish made of Sheffield plate, and many of these useful objects were later made in Sheffield when they became considerably cheaper. After 1800 they had a high domed cover which was less attractive.

All these different objects were made separately and, from the later half of the eighteenth century,

TOP *a beautifully pierced chafing dish with a spirit burner by Boulton and Fothergill, Birmingham, 1773–1774. It is quite different from the earlier type and more like an Irish dish ring in many ways.*
ABOVE *is a detail of the handle*

TOP RIGHT *a compote bowl by Tiffany and Co., New York, c 1854–5. The base shows an excellent example of a key pattern border, the bowl is engraved with amorials and the decoration is applied*

RIGHT *an Irish Georgian dish ring pierced with a fox, dog, exotic birds, flowers and scroll work, Dublin; c 1760*

52

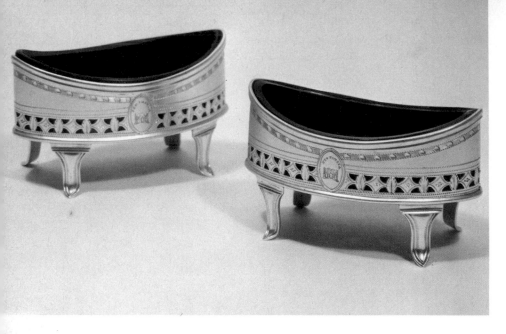

LEFT *two salt cellars by John Wren, London; 1799–1801 (see page 44)*

BELOW *an American covered bowl by John Burt (1691–1745)*

RIGHT *a Charles II silver-gilt plate, London; 1681*

FOLLOWING PAGES *a superb circular salver by Paul Storr, 1800 (see Chapter 5) and a set of four salts also by Paul Storr; 1805*

TOP *a George II oval soup tureen by John Edwards; 1737. Notice the marine motif which was fairly common; there is a crab on the lid and dolphins on the bowl*

ABOVE *an American sauceboat by Benjamin Burt; (1729–1805)*

RIGHT *a tureen by Paul de Lamerie; 1723*

en suite, in magnificent dinner services which also included meat platters of all sizes, dinner plates and dessert plates, often with a wavy rim and frequently gadrooned, with the family crest engraved at the top. Such services continued to be made at least until Victorian times; Paul Storr created a service for Buckingham Palace which is still used on State occasions.

Nevertheless, the meat served upon them required several small objects that are keenly collected today. Skewers, strong and heavy for their size, *c.* 1750–1850, tapering on a triangular plan to a sharp point, with ring or shell top, were capable of considerable variation. They were not insignificant, and the family crest was engraved upon them, but the size varies; the smallest ones, used for game, are now keenly searched out as letter openers. Marrow scoops are also popular. They usually have a long narrow scoop at one end and a broader one at the other, although the changes could be rung with a spoon or even a fork at one end. They span the years from Queen Anne to Victoria and were made in all the provincial centres in addition to London, so that marks can also be interesting and varied. Cheese scoops, shovel-shaped, with a handle rarely made of silver, were another Victorian item on the table. When the great joint was brought to the table the carvers, laid alongside, were placed on knife rests, to spare the cloth. In England, these attractive little objects are only likely to be found as part of a job lot at a sale or somewhere at the back of a drawer, but they are worth seeking for they take up little space and are inexpensive and varied, despite being no more than a strip of thick wire joining cast supports at either end

TOP *pepperpot, sauceboat, ladle and pot with finial and beaded edges by Paul Revere, American; c 1785*

ABOVE *a pair of American 19th century Empire style sauceboats by Anthony Rasch, Philadelphia; 1808–19*

RIGHT *a silver-gilt butter cooler by Paul Storr; 1816*

TOP *a punch ladle with a plain shell bowl and silver mounted whalebone handle, English; 1745.*
CENTRE *a Queen Anne basting spoon with an oval rat tail bowl and tubular handle by William Fawdery, English; 1704*
BELOW *a marrow scoop, 1775, showing a beautiful set of marks*

RIGHT *(left to right) a fiddle pattern fish slice, 1811. The pierced blade depicts a coach and four pulling up at a tollgate. Fish slice with six tapering teeth, 1800. Victorian fish servers; piercing and engraving shows pike and other fish swimming, 1857. Fish slice by Hester Bateman, 1782, pierced and engraved with bright cut engraving.*
TOP *fish slice, 1773; notice pierced fish in the blade and leafy terminal*

which may take any form, with animals as favourites. In America, where table manners dictate putting the knife down before taking a bite, these rests are more common and modern ones are sold by the dozen. Variety is such that they still make a good collection.

Long-handled serving spoons designed so that the Georgian servant, unwashed for all his finery, need not lean too close as he served the vegetables, also appeared at table, but the basting spoon was intended for kitchen use. These survive from the seventeenth century, the most distinctive type, 1690 to 1710, having a long, tapering, tubular stem, usually faceted,

ending in a baluster knop, the tube slimming towards a rat-tail bowl that is often steep sided, squarish to start with, but becoming oval later. These spoons continued to be made of heavy silver, but are less distinctive once the handle came into line with other spoons of the period.

Fish was served in a special dish, called a mazarin, fitted with a pierced strainer inside, delightfully varied but hard to find. Fish slices, on the other hand, made from about 1740 onwards, come up for sale regularly, in a variety of shapes, the most usual a broad, tapering knife blade with a shaped end,

ABOVE *a rare American toast rack by Carey Dunn, New York; c 1790. The octagonal open work platform has beaded borders*

RIGHT *the epergne gave plenty of scope for rococo decoration; this one is by John Moore, Dublin; c 1740. The curving incised lines on the dishes are typically Irish*

although the trowel, more usually a cake or short-bread slice, is also known. These were sometimes engraved but more often pierced, the design, totally at the craftsman's whim, normally including fish in one form or another. Handles, when also of silver, sometimes continued the theme, although more often they were plain. During Victorian times pairs of fish servers replaced these slices, a broad four- or five-pronged fork supplementing a slice that, while unmistakably for fish, is much nearer to a knife in shape. These were very ornately decorated and are very popular.

Piercing is the dominant feature of fruit or cake baskets, made from about 1730 onwards, although some Victorian examples, usually made in Sheffield, were solid, as were a very few of the oblong types made between 1780 and 1825. Changes in style as the basket evolved seem unimportant when all make such a delightful centrepiece on the table, whether filled with fruit or allowed to show off their workmanship to the full. Paul de Lamerie, probably England's greatest exponent of rococo, put some of

his loveliest work into these baskets, the swing handles and pierced sides showing his brilliance, and the base, solid and almost invariably engraved with armorials, being of heavy gauge silver.

Hand bells, intended originally to summon the servant, and later the family, to table, are rare in England, presumably because it was usual for at least some of the servants to remain in the room throughout the meal. Those that survive date from George I and are usually of the conventional shape, but in the States, where there is an active society for the collection of bells, they appear in the most delightful variety from about 1800 onwards. Very often the actual bell is silver plated, the handle, usually the greater part of the whole, being made of sterling silver. These handles may take almost any form, from a seated cherub or pirouetting ballet dancer to any variety of stylized decoration. A lady's long dress, naturally, makes an excellent bell and some appear like the old German wager cup, though the bells were naturally very varied. These make an unusual, inexpensive and amusing subject for collection.

Tankards and Drinking Vessels

OLD DRINKING VESSELS · TWO HANDLED CUPS · BEAKERS · TANKARDS · MUGS
PUNCH BOWLS · STRAINERS · SUGAR BOXES · PUNCH & TODDY LADLES · CORKSCREWS
NAPKIN RINGS · TUMBLER CUPS · COASTERS
WINE COOLERS & WINE CISTERNS · FOUNTAINS & URNS · FUNNELS · WINE LABELS · EWERS
BEER & CLARET JUGS · WATER JUGS

A whole chapter could be written on man's earliest drinking vessels, the horn, the coconut and other natural cups, some of which have survived because the rich had them magnificently mounted in silver, thus preserving them. They often have fascinating background stories, and are well worth a museum visit. Porringers or caudle cups (Chapter II) were also at their most interesting during the Restoration period when they were jolly and fat without much finesse in their workmanship. They sobered up before Queen Anne's time, losing their bulbous sides, spirited embossing and caryatid handles, which were all replaced with a deep band of spiral fluting above the small rim base and plain or beaded 'S' scroll handles. From this grew the two-handled cup, still a favourite for presentations, the cover rising to a fluted dome and finial. An alternative was cut-card acanthus decoration (a formal pattern of leaves cut out from sheet silver and applied with solder) around the lower part and on the lid, sometimes with gadroons or flutes around the base, which grew taller as the cup evolved, until in about 1730 the plain cup with a moulded mid-band and either harp or scroll handles emerged. The Irish delighted in harp handles and used them repeatedly, but they are not a specifically Irish feature and could be found on silver made anywhere. The two-handled cup continued on through the centuries, taking all forms of decoration as it went, but, except on presentation night, it is no longer used for drinking.

The rich man, sitting close to the Salt in the great hall, also used the most delightful silver wine cups until 1673, when glass replaced them in England. These wine cups almost always on a tall baluster stem, were charmingly decorated with light engraving or *repoussé* decoration, often leaves and flowers, their elegant lines recalled in the shapes of every wine glass known today. Nothing could be more different from the monumental sculptured steeple cup, so formal in all its ways, made at the same time.

The beaker, developed from the horn by the Saxons, was also made prolifically, particularly in east-coast towns which had strong connections with Scandinavia, where it originated. In London and Norwich these tall, tapering, cylindrical cups with a slightly everted lip, were most popular in Elizabethan times, though they were actually made for 200 years, becoming shorter and wider proportionately, often with embossed decoration during the Restoration period and quite plain throughout the eighteenth century. The normal Elizabethan cup was engraved with interlacing strapwork enclosing formal arabesques (a stylized band of scrolling foliage, seen on most Elizabethan work) with a leaf and flower motif hanging from the intersection. This form continued to be made throughout most of the seventeenth century in Aberdeen, where, rather surprisingly, they

LEFT *a tankard by Gabriel Felling of Somerset, dated 1683. This relatively unknown smith was particularly good at tankards; notice the fine engraving*

69

ABOVE LEFT *a tankard by John Haslier, New York, 1750. The raised, flat dome and the beaded rat tail on the handle are the only features typical of a New York tankard. Good* example of a corkscrew thumb-piece. ABOVE RIGHT *a tankard by Johannes Nys, Philadelphia; c 1720*

OPPOSITE LEFT *a Charles II tankard; c 1680*

were decorated more lavishly, following the Dutch style, even when made expressly for use in the Scottish kirk which preferred simplicity.

A close link existed between the kirk in Scotland and the church in Colonial America, one mutual custom being the dual-purposed cup used in the home and taken to church when needed, including, among other vessels, the low round dram cup, a very early New England piece, or the quaiche, a Scottish shallow bowl with two flat lugs as handles. But the beaker was the favourite and Boston goldsmiths set to work as soon as they were established to fill the need. Some that survive were squat, some undecorated but of the Elizabethan line, while others were similar to those made in Aberdeen, complete with the usual cast foot. By 1680 or thereabouts, they were also being made in New York, where the tall, elegant form reached its peak—eight inches in the case of one by Cornelius van der Burch (*c.* 1653–99), engraved with the words 'Robert Sanderson, 1685' confusing it with the Boston goldsmith. This and another by Jurian Blanck, Jnr (1645–1714) are engraved all over in the true Dutch style, allegorical pictures supplementing the formal leaves and flowers

with a band of stamped out foliate decoration just above the base. This is a purely New York feature seen most frequently on their fine tankards. Beakers continued to be made for more than a century; Paul Revere (1735–1818) produced one in 1795, but like most things their shape changed with the years and lost its basic elegance.

The tankard was also taken to church in America, and was often soberly inscribed with the initials of both husband and wife who regarded it as a tangible proof of their marriage vows. In England, tankards had been concerned with intemperance, at a very early stage; the Peg Tankard was devised in order to limit the amount each man drank. They were taken to Denmark by the Vikings, and returned to north-eastern towns as a Scandinavian speciality by 1660. The Scots so preferred claret to beer that very few tankards were made before the eighteenth century, and even tea drinking established itself with difficulty, eventually supplanting claret as a national drink.

The Elizabethan tankard was tall and narrow like a flagon, then in the reign of James I it became much shorter, with a flat lid protruding in front to a point.

RIGHT AND BELOW *a tankard with lion thumb-piece by John Backe; 1701*

FOLLOWING PAGES *a pair of George III beer jugs by John Peyne, London; 1767*

During the Commonwealth it was often skirted at the base, became drum-shaped and had one low step to its flat lid, which gradually grew in height during the century, becoming double stepped but still flat by about 1675. Armorials were almost invariably engraved in a cartouche consisting of feathers and scrolls, and the thumbpiece was double scrolled or twin lobed on ordinary examples, with occasionally a lion couchant guarding the lid of something finer. The whole body was raised from a single sheet of silver, and applied mouldings, usually plain but occasionally in the form of twisted rope, strengthened the base. The 'C' scroll handle was cast very occasionally with a tapering line of beads running down it, known as a beaded rat-tail, and other applied mouldings. occurred on the handles of some provincial tankards. During the last ten years of the century acanthus leaf or spiral flutes were sometimes embossed above the base rim or, for a rather longer period, Chinese patterns (known as *'chinoiserie'* decoration) were engraved all over. With these exceptions English tankards were decorated only with engraved armorials between 1660 and 1800, very occasionally cut-card applications strengthening the joints of the

handles. If other ornamentation is present it has been added later, unless the tankard is mounted on three pomegranate or ball and claw feet. In this case it will probably have a thumbpiece to match and eight equally placed pegs inside, and will have been made in Hull or York where many such peg tankards were embossed all over.

Another invariable rule is that a drum-shaped tankard without a lid is an incomplete article, for the seventeenth-century mug was a small bulbous vessel with a reeded neck. During the eighteenth century, the mug (which, unlike tankards, never had a lid) was much closer in shape to the covered vessel, but was usually larger, holding up to a gallon or more, while the mug rarely exceeds one pint in capacity.

During the eighteenth century the tankard gradually moved away from the drum-shape, becoming round and somewhat bulging, usually with a moulded

BELOW *a good example of a Boston tankard with an acorn shaped finial on the domed cover, by Samuel Edwards, Boston; c 1760*

RIGHT *some examples of different wine labels; the bat-shaped Sherry label is very unusual and notice Mr Punch and his dog in the 'P' for port (see page 80)*

band around the widest part, while the thumbpiece took a more open form. The manner in which the shape evolved is unimportant, but the round dome started to rise in Queen Anne's reign, the foot matching it a little more slowly, until, c. 1780–1820, a flat-topped reeded type was made, never very popular, but of superb quality.

Any suggestion that American silver merely copies the English can be refuted at once by looking at American tankards. The drum-shape was used, and occasionally remained plain in New England, although more often the step of the flat lid was gadrooned, the thumbpiece imaginative, and the shield at the base of the handle applied with a well-cast mask such as a dolphin or cherub. This shape was maintained at least fifty years longer than in England, eventually growing so that height was gained on a more narrow, tapering, but still straight-sided tankard, only rarely encircled by a moulded band, and with a high domed lid. This was quite unlike any in England. It was 1750–60 before the baluster form was used, and even later in Philadelphia, where the double scroll handle was a speciality. Occasionally, throughout the century, a high finial surmounted the dome on Boston's tankards (and once, c. 1710, on a flat cover), but only rarely on those made elsewhere. This was never an English feature, but one or two were made c. 1720–30.

The New York tankard first appeared in about 1690, some twenty years after the earliest known tankards from Boston, and were immediately distinguished by a narrow band of stamped out ornament above the moulded baseband, itself deeper than usual in England, over which a narrow zig-zagging strip was applied, called a meander wire. For so small a feature the effect is considerable. These tankards have the usual plain body with engraved armorials, and the lid, stepped more squarely than in England, has a protruding flange, usually covered in engraving which was repeated on the flat part of the lid, into which coins were sometimes inset. The thumbpiece is usually corkscrew in shape, with considerable ornamentation surrounding the hinge. On the handle itself, just below the hinge, a lion couchant is apt to take his ease. The whole handle may be covered in applied cast ornamentation in high relief, but coin inset is a particular New York feature. Finally, the shield at the tip of the handle invariably carries a fine applied mask. The whole effect is magnificent. Such tankards really demonstrate just how different American silver can be, but as in England, tankards ceased to be fashionable during the nineteenth century. Even mugs were for children, holding less than half a pint, usually with plenty of embossed

decoration which was often very appropriate, such as boys playing football. Handles were strongly cast and fanciful, a twisted leafy spray perhaps, with a snake slithering around it, its head, ready to strike, as thumbpiece. A look at any sale catalogue dealing with this period will show that craftsmen also kept themselves busy decorating old silver articles, including tankards, as 'embossed later', or words to that effect, appear frequently.

Punch, almost a fetish in England between 1680 and 1760, was never fashionable in America, but several punch bowls were made in Boston. John Coney created at least two of the Montieth type (with notched rims, removable in England after 1695). One, *c.* 1700–10, with a fixed rim, is as elaborate and richly ornamented as any in England, the other, *c.* 1715–22, is quite unadorned except for engraved armorials, the detachable rim uncluttered. Bowls that could well serve punch were also made after 1750, lower and wider than those in England, but lightly decorated and quite glorious. Original punch bowls fetch very high prices now but the ritual required several supporting pieces of silver, some of which are more within the range of the small collector.

Strainers, for the orange or lemon juice used in punch, needed to be large enough to rest across the rim of the bowl, giving the imaginative craftsman immense scope, both in the piercing of the straining part and in the formation of the handles. The straining part in early pieces had small holes punched to a pattern and the later ones had the designs cut out. The handles could take any form into which silver could be twisted; it could be pierced like the handle of an American porringer, or decorated with rococo motifs applied to a solid lug.

Castors to contain the sugar and spice that went into punch also came to table, but before sugar was sufficiently refined a box was used, as it had been since the early-sixteenth century when sugar was found to improve the very rough wine. Such boxes, usually in museums now, took many forms, the shell being a favourite motif. Coiled serpent handles were also popular and when these boxes were made in New England, in the first years of the eighteenth century, the snake still writhed himself into a loop on their lids. One by John Coney also had the time-honoured lobes around the sides of the box, and was raised on four feet, as so many English examples had been. Those by Edward Winslow incorporated the gadroons he so loved among a wealth of fine ornament.

Punch ladles make a delightful subject for collection, with their fanciful silver heads mounted on an ivory, wood or whalebone handle. They were con-

siderably smaller than those made for soup, the scoop formed like any sort of shell, flower, bell, or just a simple oval with a lip at either end. Those intended for toddy in Scotland (whisky with hot water), as any small ladle bearing Scottish marks in the punch period would be, were usually of the simpler form, and these continued to be made in every corner of Scotland, the fashion for whisky never having suffered the fate of punch. Their varied marking gives an additional interest to collectors.

The bottle, itself a rough piece of glass, required a coaster to stand on to protect the table from scratches and drips. It also needed a label to identify its contents, a funnel for decanting the wine, and a corkscrew.

TOP LEFT *a can by Bancroft Woodcock, Delaware; c 1760*

BELOW LEFT *a large American tankard by Myer Myers, New York; c 1770. A good example of an openwork thumb-piece*

Only the corkscrew is still necessary today, but it can take interesting forms particularly in America and Canada where figural silver became such a charming art in about 1820. Since the hand must be able to grip a corkscrew, as it can, for instance, the shape of a pheasant walking, the design was restricted in a way which does not apply to the design of, let us say, napkin rings, a subject of immense scope for the imagination. They can include models of children driving a dog-cart, the ring as the load; children on a see-saw, the ring balanced centrally; a bride and groom with an outsize ring between them, or anything else that illustrates human or animal life. They really are fun.

BELOW *a small montieth bowl by Isaac Dighton, 1700*

ABOVE *an American octagonal bowl, c 1800, not typical of the early New York bowls. A pair of American cups by William G Forbes, New York; c 1810. The circular feet are decorated with a narrow band of stiff leafage*

The modern silversmith, once more an artist, has taken many objects known through the ages, and given them new form, but in a recent American competition for design in silver, a first prize was won for a wine bottle with two cups. This elegant bottle is shaped like a skittle in a bowling alley, with a round silver stopper chased with human bodies in a naturalistic way. The cups, like teacups without handles, bring the old tumbler cup to mind, for although those were straight-sided they were also without handles, and usually without ornament, except for armorials or, occasionally, acanthus leaf decoration around the lower half. Beaten up from a single sheet of thick silver, with balancing weight in the base so that the upright position is always maintained, they were at their best during the eighteenth century and were made in all sizes from quite tiny to three or four inches in height, in all parts of England, making them a good medium for collecting provincial marks.

Coasters, or decanter stands, were made roughly from 1760 to 1830 in pairs or larger sets, and mostly have a turned wooden base covered in green baize, so that they can be pushed along the table without scratching it. Superior models may have tiny ivory balls that run smoothly, and the very superior are mounted on a wagon that can be pulled along, itself a fine piece of silver. During the neo-classic period these coasters were pierced, geometrically, classically, or with festoons of cast husks, medallions, swags or scrolls applied over simple bar piercing. The Irish, naturally, were more imaginative, and anything considered suitable for a dish ring could be cut, chased or embossed upon the coasters: scrolls, flowers, leaves or trees forming the background for farmyard animals, foxes, dogs, game birds or figures. Sometimes coasters had corded borders, but the rim could be finished off with mouldings of any sort, scalloped, everted or nicely undulating. After 1790 piercing died out, having first been combined in small amounts with light engraving. Then the coasters' sides became more shaped, while heavy embossing, usually in vine motifs with gadrooned borders, became usual. Sometimes, around the turn of the century, they carried no decoration, and when straight-sided could be rather severe, although of an interesting shape which made them very attractive. The earliest coasters were quite small and definitely intended for bottles, the larger ones accommodating decanters. These stands look lovely on a sideboard today, even those made in Sheffield from machine-made parts, which are considerably cheaper, or those in Sheffield plate, which in the early days was of superior workmanship.

TOP *a George III wine coaster made by Benjamin Smith; 1807*

CENTRE *a George II punch ladle*

ABOVE *a soup ladle by Paul Revere, Boston; c 1785. The handle is engraved with a bright-cut wrigglework border framed by one of a simple zigzag design*

Wine coolers, which do well for flowers, or as ice buckets today, were intended for cooling the single bottle of wine during the late-eighteenth and early-nineteenth centuries, and should not be confused with the wine cistern. Coolers were made from about 1665 to 1850, becoming even bigger and grander, with more magnificent sculpture, as men tried to prove their wealth, in competition from the time that Charles II had one made for his mistress weighing 1,000 oz, to the final winner, an 8,000 oz bath by Charles Kandler, *c.* 1739. They were used at banquets, when dozens of bottles lay in them on a bed of ice, and they concern the small collector no more than the wine fountain, sculptured urns, sixteenth-century steeple cups or salts.

The urns contained wine in those days, but when the wine was bottled a funnel became necessary, and this was made in silver from early-Georgian times. These funnels are still useful today, and although there is no great variety, they are usually of good quality and therefore pleasing. Most are made in combination with a strainer, with a separate pierced bowl, either fitting inside that of the main body or screwing into the stem itself, which curves out to an

ABOVE *a pair of American cans by Myer Myers, New York; c 1750*

RIGHT *a large Victorian helmet-shaped ewer by Robert Garrard; 1868*

FOLLOWING PAGES: *left, an American two-handled cup by Jacob Hurd (1702–1758) engraved with the coat of arms of a merchant of Boston*
right, an American tankard, New York, 1674–1757 by Cornelius Kierstede

open mouth at its end, so deflecting the flow of wine gently down the side of the bottle or decanter. Very few are decorated beyond the engraving of arms or a crest, but a gadrooned, tongue and dart, or other border is usual, while some have a hook-like lug for hanging over a punch bowl.

Any wine lotion or other beverage could be put into the same type of bottle in the early days, and silver bottle tickets, later known as wine labels, were made for identification purposes from about 1730, although few are found now which were made before the seventies. At that time a whole new class of people were drinking wine in great variety, while hardly knowing the difference between arquebuscade, a healing lotion for gunshot wounds, and claret, which made some sort of labelling essential. This is a specialist subject, with clubs to join and many technical and interesting books to read. The collector of wine labels can gain extra pleasure by the discovery of what the various names denote, and will perhaps need a dictionary or recipe book. The early labels were hand-made from thick silver in a variety of shapes. They were usually plain, with a thread, wriggle work, or gadrooned border and the name of the wine pierced or engraved in bold letters filling the centre. Others were chased with trailing vine

tendrils, leaves and grapes as far back as 1735 or so, when Sandilands Drinkwater was the chief, if not the only maker. Such hand-made labels were produced up to 1860, particularly in London, where a family crest could make an outstanding contribution to design, and in Scotland, where solid good workmanship came naturally.

The majority of labels, however, were die stamped and made on rather thinner silver during the first forty years of the nineteenth century, and bore very varied marks. In 1784 Matthew Linwood had perfected this method in Birmingham and although they tried, others were unable to match the skill and precision with which he cut his casts in steel, and the consequent sharpness of the finished silver article. The shapes such labels took is limited only by the imagination, since the basic form of a surface on which a name can be pierced or engraved can be decorated and transformed in an infinite number of ways. The surface need not even be plain, for on the labels in the shapes of the shell and the vine leaf, to take just two examples, the name of the wine can be either cut out, or superimposed over the textured model. Nor is the whole name always spelled out: quite frequently P, C or S appear for Port, Claret, or Sherry, while at other times the label consists just of the outlined

initial, in scrolled or plain form—perhaps an M for Madeira, or a W for Whisky, hanging from a chain. These labels must be really sharp for some were made in a mould after 1810, characterized by lack of brilliance. They are considerably less valuable and should not be mistaken for the superior type.

Paper labels on bottles became law in 1860, killing the production of silver tickets, but standards had been declining for twenty years by then. In their heyday they were made by most of the finest makers, such as Paul Storr, Phipps and Robinson, or Hester Bateman (whose labels will be about double the price of the others even though she is not of the same class) in London; John Teare, John Tweedie or Benjamin Tait in Dublin; Linwood or Joseph Willmore, among many others, in Birmingham.

Jugs, or ewers, among the most useful pieces of antique silver today, have been made from earliest times, but one might as well finance a moon landing as collect original ewers. Yet these ewers and their fine basins, usually twenty or more inches across, were also made during the nineteenth and early-twentieth centuries, in their original forms, high classical, or helmet-shaped, the later ones being less ornate and embossed in very high relief. The earliest collectable jugs (for the very rich) were intended for beer, those of Queen Anne's time being pear-shaped, of superlative quality and decorated only with engraved armorials, although occasionally a little cut-card-work surrounded the small applied pouring lip. Sometimes these jugs were covered, more often not, and they were set on a low round foot, which grew taller as the century advanced; they also had a

TOP LEFT *one of a pair of wine coolers, made in New York; c 1840*

LEFT *an American covered jug made in Baltimore; c 1834*

RIGHT *an American flagon chased to simulate oak; c 1850*

FOLLOWING PAGES: *left, a peg tankard by William Ramsey, Newcastle, 1670, which shows the features of Northern English work (see page 73)*

RIGHT *late Victorian silver-gilt ewer with blue enamelled motifs; Edinburgh, 1850*

ABOVE *an American circular bowl, c 1785 which may have been used for punch. It shows how initials were used after 1783 in the place habitually used by armorials*

RIGHT *an American wine cooler in the Neo-classical style, made by Tiffany and Co.; c 1865*

FOLLOWING PAGES: *left, two Harlequin taper sticks, one with an extinguisher, 1765–6 (see page 117)*
right, American chocolate pot by Zachariah Brigden, mid 18th century. It shows the moulinet or stirring rod taking the place of the finial and attached by its chain to the handle

well-made C scroll handle, possibly leaf capped, and a plain rim. Not many such jugs were made in America, where they had a domed lid, like a Georgian tankard, and a considerably more ambitious handle, but plenty were made in *art nouveau* style.

The wine jug, which is all silver, and the claret jug, made of glass with silver mounts, both appeared in the mid-nineteenth century, water (apparently) having been the accepted drink in the years between, say, 1765 and 1840.

Water pitchers were very much the same as they are today, with their broad pear-shape easing out to a wide lip, the rim, strengthened by applied mouldings curving down and up again to the start of a simple reeded handle, all set on a circular base. They had solid good quality, with no frills, such as can be found on a wine jug, and were usable for any liquid.

Although occasionally of pear-shape jugs more often took the high classical form, with a narrow neck surmounting a vase-shaped body set on a high foot, usually with a high classical handle. Decoration was not confined to classical motifs (although those in America, which were even more heavily decorated, are inclined to be), and the decorations may take any form such as scenes from mythology, sea themes, and the usual nature studies. Stoppers give a great chance for originality, ranging from formal designs to depictions of mermaids, or foxes craning their necks to see what is going on. Most of these jugs are embossed (engraving, which began to be used in about 1860, looks very flat and insipid), but some are basically plain and overlaid with very high cast ornament which can be most attractive. This can also occur on claret jugs when foliage and flowers encircle the hips of a fine glass jug before twisting themselves into the start of the handle. Mounts on these jugs range from a fairly simple lip, handle and stopper to something altogether more ambitious, the glass itself making a beautiful contribution to an altogether lovely object.

ABOVE *this silver mounted glass Claret jug by L H Stockwell, London, 1880, is a beautiful example of Victorian work*

RIGHT *American pitcher by S Kirk and Son, Baltimore; c 1860. The two workmen were famous for their ornate silver. This oviform pitcher is repousse with hunting scenes*

96

After Dinner Silver

When the ladies left the gentlemen at the dining table in Georgian times, they settled down to their tea table and happy chatter. Today the formal after-dinner drink is coffee, but since the finest teasets first made c. 1785 included a coffee pot it is reasonable to suppose that coffee always had been an alternative choice.

Coffee and hot chocolate, as drinks, came to England well before 1650, when the coffee house became such a fashionable meeting place. Chocolate pots were made in the same style as those for coffee but with one important difference. The finial is either removable, or has a second small aperture on top, generally hinged, through which a swizzle stick, called a molionet, can be inserted, to beat the chocolate to a froth. This is the only true distinction that can determine the original use of the pot. In England the handle was usually set at right angles to the spout between 1705 and 1715, continuing a little later in America, although rarely as late as 1720–35, when Charles le Roux (1689–1745) made his well-known New York coffee pot. This is of the English Queen Anne style and of superb weight and proportion: tall (eleven inches), of tapering cylindrical shape, it was set on a tightly fitting moulded base, with a high domed round cover and turned finial, higher than the contemporary English baluster knop.

One important difference is that English side-handle pots have a simple thumbpiece on the cover above the hinge which joins the lid to the handle socket, while le Roux's does not. The spout in both cases was strengthened by a plain round disc of silver at the joint, except when cut-card-work was used, which added greatly to the value. On this New York pot the spout itself is round, completely straight and sawn off at the top, a style which was in use before 1 90 in England and occasionally again during the years 1725–35 when the domed cover had disappeared. The spout in England was curved gracefully, the lower lip projecting well beyond the upper, over which more often than not a hinged cover was fitted. This was either round or faceted, frequently octagonal like many of the pots themselves, and evolved into the cast 'duck's head' spout, its mouth explaining the term, that lasted until about 1725. Zacharia Brigden (Boston, 1734–87) made a chocolate pot in this form well after the turn of the century, its octagonal duck's head spout boldly faceted and the body identical in every way except for the chain connecting the removable tip of the finial to the hinge panel.

Up until about 1730 coffee pots were decorated only with armorials, opposite the handle when it was set at right angles, otherwise on the side. Even during the thirties, when some pots carried a little flat chasing (but not embossing), the majority were still plain, with the occasional exception of cut-card-work, or (rarely) flutes on the domed lid. Any pot decorated

PREVIOUS PAGES: *left, a chocolate pot by Edward Winslow, American; c 1700.*
RIGHT *an American coffee pot and sugar bowl by Simeon Sonmain; c 1730*

LEFT *this baluster jug has all the best features of the Queen Anne period and is by Robert Cooper; 1708*

LEFT *a sweetmeat basket by Daniel Fueter, American; c 1765*

BELOW *a salver by Myer Myers, American; c 1760–70*

RIGHT *a salver by Paul Revere made in 1760 and 12 inches in diameter*

ABOVE *a George II tapering cylindrical coffee pot by Edward Feline; 1733*

BELOW *a rare Irish chocolate pot by Ralph Woodhouse, Dublin; c 1735*

otherwise before 1740, therefore, has been later 'improving', to its detriment. Even during the rococo period, 1740 to 1760, when the decoration of most objects was taken for granted, the majority of coffee pots remained unadorned, although overall embossing of rococo scrolls and shells were perfectly in order, as were *chinoiserie* designs. This Chinese style could be extremely fascinating, and usually had a well-balanced mixture of scrolling curves, leaves and flowers, and Chinese figures in many different poses— sitting with parasols, strumming mandolins, fishing, strolling by the water's edge and generally amusing themselves. A Chinese figure also serves as finial on the cover. A coffee pot that is embossed all over with flowers is probably Victorian, for although flowers were used during the rococo period, they were never overcrowded and left good clear surfaces of silver unadorned. Strangely, for standards of decoration in this period were very high, the plain coffee pot has a greater value.

During the late twenties the domed cover was flattened out to form a flat-topped or stepped dome, and the straight-sided cylindrical pot gave way to the 'tucked under' form, its straight round sides curving gracefully at the bottom to sit on a wider rimmed base. This evolved into the baluster, or pear form, and the change was complete by about 1750.

In the meantime the hot water jug, with its small applied lip, which sometimes had a hinged cover, was made and decorated in the same manner as the coffee or chocolate pot, although the value is always less. However, the Queen Anne hot water jug illustrated here, is a beautiful example of that later baluster style, and is of superb quality, with lovely cut-card-work surrounding the joints. This shape was still being used in the late fifties. The chief difference as the eighties approached was in the height, for the foot rose considerably to give an effect of slender grace rather than solid quality. From about 1760 to 1780 gadroons on the foot and rim became a positive feature, complemented by the swirling grooves normally found on the accompanying finial, which itself varied within the limits of the shapes of acorns, flames, pineapples etc. It is the spout that carried the main decoration on these pots; it was strong, with deep swirling flutes, cast applications and other

RIGHT *an American coffee urn with bright-cut engraving; c 1808*

101

ABOVE *a pair of filigree sweetmeat baskets by Peter Cunard with ladles by Paul Storr*

LEFT *a small Commonwealth dish, maker's mark HN with a bird below, London, 1657*

RIGHT *a pair of Louis XV candelabra by Etienne Jacques Mare, Paris, 1733*

FOLLOWING PAGES *two coffee pots dated 1765 and 1769 with scroll decorated spouts*

ABOVE AND RIGHT *silver and silver-gilt candlestick and candle holders by Stuart Devlin, London, 1972. The candles* ABOVE *are set in gold filigree lamp-shades and* RIGHT *silver-gilt points set in silver baskets lie between each candle. These points can be lifted out and fruit or anything else can be put in the baskets instead. The base is entirely articulated so that the whole centre piece can be pushed into any shape you like*

ABOVE *a Queen Anne small, plain, octagonal pear-shaped hot milk jug by Richard Raine; 1713*

RIGHT *a highly decorated American coffee pot; c 1830*

FOLLOWING PAGES: *left, inkstand by John Coney, (1655–1722), Boston, early 18th century.*
right a complete set of James I Apostle spoons, known as the Sulhamstead set, by the unknown maker 'IS', London; 1617–1618. It is one of only five sets known made by a single maker within the same year. The gilded figures on the spoons show the apostolic emblems according to the Germanic system and include in the nimbus of each a dove, symbolic of the Holy Ghost

rococo features. On decorated pots these features are less obvious because of lack of contrast. The spout was still cast strongly when the first swags and garlands appeared, embossed in restrained amounts on the same style of pot. This changed radically in about 1780, and took the graceful classical line seen on American sugar urns—a vase surmounted by an elegantly waisted spool neck. At first classical motifs were embossed upon these, the effect made lighter by beaded borders, but engraving never before seen on coffee pots except as armorials quickly became the accepted decoration, almost invariably in restrained bright cut.

Before this period differences in America were few; embossed decoration when used was restrained;

spouts intricate and gadroons much in evidence. Finials were rather higher and much more varied but overall shape if occasionally somewhat higher was virtually the same. During the classical period the gallery surrounding the shoulders of the pot on some Philadelphian examples is their outstanding feature, while beaded borders, as used in that city, continued to be distinctive and easy to recognize but difficult to pinpoint.

The classical was the last definable new style. The majority of coffee pots from about 1810 were made *en suite* with a teaset, in any of the revival styles or in any shape or mode of decoration that best suited the rest of the set, and ranged from the elegant to the absurd. But whatever the style and date of the pot it is virtually certain that tea or coffee cups would have been passed by a liveried servant to the assembled company on a salver, really the same thing as a waiter, although that word is more often applied to the smaller examples.

Of all objects these have been used the most consistently through the years, for even now that servants no longer abound it is still easier to pass drinks on a tray than individually. Trays, however, did not appear before 1790 and were large and heavy, with two handles, oval or rectangular and usually set on four feet. In those days decoration was light, with bright cut engraving and perhaps a pierced rim; a thread, or light gadrooned border were early variants, with nothing but armorials engraved centrally although before long the border becomes heavily gadrooned or applied with heavy cast decoration. The centre flat was chased or engraved after 1850. They can be magnificent things, standing on display on the sideboard on their cast shell feet, but are not practical to carry around.

The earliest salvers date from the period of Queen Anne and rather before, and are set on a capstan (trumpet-shaped) foot and have a reeded or gadrooned rim. They are most often found in collections of church plate, but the square salver with corners shaped in many ways was set on three or four bracket feet and what follows developed from this. Feet, as time went on, were cast in endless ways usually in keeping with the salver's border which was its main feature. The border rises above the flat surface on the salver and is often cast and applied, but it can be hammered up in one piece with only the feet being cast separately. Essentially these lovely things are very plain, and throughout every period of greater ornamentation many are still made in the old forms, the main surface depending on engraved armorials for interest. In about 1730 the round shape developed

and from about 1734 no more were made square until the era of reproductions. The 'Chippendale' or 'piecrust' border, a moulded form of reversing curves, or the 'Bath', with brackets replacing the curves, were very popular. They easily evolved into the scroll and shell border which during the high rococo period became cast borders of great intricacy. Sometimes masks—carved faces set in shields—were set in the borders. Yet in 1760 it was to the simple forms that borders returned, with gadrooned rims. This lasted well into the nineteenth century. The shell at junctions was occasionally retained and varied by beaded, thread or other simple themes. During the rococo period *flat chasing* on the main surface was also used, in swirling style, usually making an outer ring of decoration, and with a modicum of clear surface surrounding the central arms engraved in rococo cartouches. This extra decoration was never *engraved* before the neo-classic period, when bright cut was in order, but ornamentation has often been added later, usually destroying the balance. The largest salvers, up to thirty inches wide and sometimes called chargers, are most impressive with heavy borders and plenty of ornament. The smaller examples, anything from six inches or less, but more often seven

to ten inches, look better when unadorned, as they have nice hoof, scroll or shell feet.

Today, when salvers rank second only to cups as sporting trophies, it is these Georgian forms that are most frequently reproduced, with the inscription recording the event in the place originally taken by arms. If the piece is antique, however, it is most probable that the arms will have been erased, making room for the inscription and thus spoiling the patina of the old silver. This happens all too often and is a point to watch. Salvers continued to be made throughout the nineteenth century, some of them ornate in typical fashion with heavy rims, pierced, or cast and applied. Flat chasing covers the inner surface and struggles for attention among the plethora of motifs, further confused by a matted background. Yet even during this period many retained the dignified border and kept generally good proportions.

Dinner was taken very early in the eighteenth century and it was quite usual for the appetite to return before bedtime, when in summer nothing could assuage it more delightfully than a dish of strawberries, as popular then as now. Of course the strawberry dish was also used for other fruit and conserves, but these simple round plates, their scalloped rims divided into fluted panels by a deep dividing rib, were most often used. Although they were made in England, the majority that survive (and they appear for sale quite regularly) are Irish, *c.* 1710–40. The size varied and the bigger ones, ten to twelve inches across, with twenty-four or thirty-two panels, were piled with the fruit to be served, while the smaller ones, anything of five inches or more, received the individual helpings, and were usually made in sets. These plates were beaten up from a single sheet of heavy silver, the scalloped edge curling up by perhaps 45°, sometimes taking a wavy contour as added refinement.

Originally they were plain except for arms engraved centrally, and remained like this in Ireland, unless they were decorated later. This is an important point to watch because, although some of the deeper type, with almost vertical sides were engraved in period (*c.* 1800–30), those 'improved' later often have the Victorian matted background.

Sweets might also be passed after dinner, daintily arranged in a sweetmeat basket, a smaller version of those described (Chapter III) for cake, pierced in all the styles of the second half of the eighteenth century. They were usually round, not more than five inches across, becoming boat-shaped later and particularly pleasant to collect, as they possess all the grace of expensive silver on a smaller scale.

LEFT *an American coffee pot by Paul Revere, Boston;
c 1795. It is 15 inches high and the plain baluster body
is engraved with initials in the contemporary script*

ABOVE *two George II candlesticks by John Cafe, 1755;
and a rare Channel Islands salver, Guernsey; c 1735*

Other objects used to hold sweets include a dainty dish that survives from the seventeenth century, small and round, not unlike the strawberry dish except that the sides are somewhat steeper, the bowl a trifle deeper, and it is made of exceptionally thin silver. Decoration consists of simple designs punched with a round headed tool and flowers and grapes were favourites with the bowl finished off by two dainty handles, or lugs, often of shell design. In America the all-purpose porringer could have been used for sweets, but a similar bowl in England, of which few survive, is thought to have been a surgeon's bleeding bowl.

In the meantime the gentlemen helped themselves to a pinch of snuff from a beautifully decorated little box with a hinged lid. Snuff boxes were made of many materials in many countries from the mid-seventeenth century onwards. The finest were French, made of gold and sometimes studded with jewels; the most collectable today are the silver boxes made in the first forty years of the nineteenth century, usually in Birmingham. Snuff boxes appear regularly today in the sale rooms of London and New York dating from about 1715, when they are generally London made. They are about three inches wide with canted corners and a border of scrolling foliage. This is a popular size, large enough to hold cigarettes. The majority made before the turn of the seventeenth century came from London and Edinburgh with a few from Ireland, and were usually of this plain-topped form, dependent on borders for decoration, although there were others much smaller and of almost every

geometrical shape. The cast top first appeared before the Queen Anne period, often depicting Biblical or mythological scenes, and no rules can be laid down even though those appearing for sale are mostly plain on top, perhaps with a crest engraved, a jewel inset or symmetrical background decoration such as basket weave. The borders and sides are decorated, bright cut engraving being used during the last fifteen years of the century.

This type of box did not cease to be made with the nineteenth century, nor did London makers fade out. Backgrounds were often engine turned, a stippled effect was used quite frequently on the sides, or on part of them, whether there was a cast or embossed top or not. Francis Clark of Birmingham was particularly fond of using engine turning and he together with Nathaniel Mills, Joseph Willmore and Matthew Linwood were the best known among many imaginative workers from that city.

It is hardly possible to discuss the decoration of nineteenth-century snuff boxes without bringing in the box-type of vinaigrette so often made by the same makers. Nathaniel Mills, for instance, specialized in lids depicting the stately homes, abbeys, castles or cathedrals of Britain (although he did make other types), strongly cast and occasionally embossed in high relief and attached to boxes that generally had strongly embossed borders and sides. A London maker of snuff boxes in the early years of the nineteenth century depicted humorous scenes from paintings, in the Hogarth manner, while sporting subjects, the countryside, deer in a park, love scenes (very rare and rather fun) or historically commemorative subjects, were others that found their way on to lids, made by a dozen or more Birmingham specialists of both snuff boxes and vinaigrettes.

Boxes for snuff, however, were rarely made after 1840 while vinaigrettes were a force until 1870 or so. The various types appeared at definite periods; commemorative decoration was inspired by Trafalgar,

LEFT *Queen Anne snuffers and stand by Andrew Raven, London; 1703*

RIGHT *an American silver waiter by Joseph and Nathaniel Richardson, Philadelphia; c 1785. The rim is beaded, the border pierced with circles linked by bars and the centre has a contemporary foliate monogram*

RIGHT *Victorian boxes from Birmingham. The largest is a casket dated 1851 by Edward Smith;* LEFT *a silver-gilt vinaigrette by Gervase Wheeler, 1838;* CENTRE *a William IV snuff-box with the lid chased in relief;* RIGHT *a rectangular vinaigrette, the lid chased with a view of York Minster*

BELOW *one of a pair of heavy George III table candlesticks by Robert Makepeace and Richard Carter; 1777. The border is gadrooned, the stem knopped and faceted and the sconce campana-shaped*

and the scenic tableaux, which were either engraved, cast or *repousse*, were in vogue from roughly 1830 to 1870. Despite the similarity of tops, these boxes are unlikely to be confused, for the average size vinaigrette was about one-and-a-half by one inch, sometimes with a suspending ring that is never found on snuff boxes. This enabled the little box to be hung somewhere on the person of the user, for a vinaigrette, originally intended to protect its owner from infection (when called a pomander, from about 2000 BC), now had the equally important task of combating the offensive odour of unwashed bodies. The tiny receptacle contained a pungent brew of spiced vinegar, soaked on a sponge, giving out its fumes through a pierced grille, inside which can be seen when the lid is opened, and is often of as fine, or finer, workmanship than that on top—being delicate, intricate and surprising.

The box type of vinaigrette was, however, only one among many, for they came in every shape and form that it was possible to reproduce in silver in miniature at any time from *c.* 1790 to *c.* 1875. Some of them were a little bigger, and were as much as three inches across when the subject merited it. Favourites among these shapes are purses, hearts, roses, coronets, shells, watches and books, although the full list would be as long as the imagination of a Birmingham craftsman.

Cards or other games were frequently played by men (and women) in the evenings, and the gamblers used counter boxes for their chips which were themselves very fine. Most boxes that appear for sale now date between 1640 and 1700, are cylindrical, no larger than the counters themselves and bear a portrait in silver of the monarch, or have something similar on top. One particularly fine box, *c.* 1670, was composed of three cylinders combined in the form of a trefoil, which contained thirty-one Charles II sixpences. Another (*c.* 1640) was filled with twenty-seven counters each engraved with a sovereign's head from William I to Charles I.

Of course the most important objects in any household were candlesticks and very great quantities were made in silver in every age. A description of their form and style at each period would be sufficient to fill a book but here it is compressed to a few basic points. Taper sticks, used in letter writing for heating the wax for the seal, also appear for sale quite frequently, following the prevailing style of candlesticks in miniature.

Candlesticks had had a very long history before the Britannia period gave the short heavy sticks of the day that special sheen. At that time, and until 1760,

they were all cast and being very good quality were difficult to damage. The various parts were each cast in two halves although no join is visible. Before *c*. 1745 the Queen Anne stick, which was almost unchanged until 1725, had a knopped, tapering, faceted stem with a distinct shoulder, a reel-shaped sconce (to hold the candle) with no nozzle (the wide rim at its top) and a moulded foot. Occasionally the foot was square but more usually circular, octagonal or hexagonal, and was sunken centrally and beautifully faceted, sometimes achieving a lovely diamond appearance. Armor-

ials are rare, but occasionally a crest appears on the sunken part of the foot. This baluster form did not change substantially through the following decades, but because of increasing ornamentation and height it may, at times, appear to have done so. Change came about gradually, with considerable variety in the shape of the base, fluted, gadrooned, or with shell decoration; stems fluted or banded, the shoulders reflecting the base or with finely chased foliage. Yet at the same time rococo ornament was finding its way in increasing amounts on to the sticks of the masters.

Shells, scrollwork, flowers, foliage, flutes and other motifs, were at their best superlative, but were sometimes heavy and overdone, and had themes jostling for space on the restricted surface.

The harlequin, or caryatid candlestick, was a most attractive variation and appeared in about 1750. It was said to be usually by John Cafe, although those seen in sales have also been by other makers. It consists of a figure, arising from a domed circular base heavy with rococo ornament, supporting the wax pan and sconce above its head. Harlequin and Columbine were favourites but the figures can be blackamoors, Grecian goddesses, Chinamen or anything similar, and are great fun.

Rococo on candlesticks, at least in restrained form, died more slowly than on some objects, shells in particular being retained until about 1770, by which time the square base had arrived, its rim and all shoulders gadrooned, or occasionally fluted. This form was still baluster-shaped, but the tall Corinthian column had also come in about 1760 exactly as it might appear in a Greek temple, the illusion being less strong when the pediment was hung with foliage and draperies than when dependent on gadrooned edges and acanthus leaves. Prices drop sharply in about 1765, when Birmingham and Sheffield first produced die stamped candlesticks, but the quality was not good for the first five years while technique improved. Die cast sticks were stamped out from very thin silver in many parts, soldered together, and filled with resin, sometimes with an iron bar up the centre, to give them weight, such candlesticks being described as 'loaded'. This method was used for virtually all those made in Birmingham and Sheffield. The candlestick makers of these cities were always to the fore in design, but because of the thin metal the die stamped variety are easily damaged, while the resin inside them makes repair difficult, so that they should be very carefully examined for faults which can quickly become worse.

With so many designs and forms of ornament, coming thick and fast as the nineteenth century progressed, the basic foundation continued to be in only three shapes, the baluster, the column and a most elegant tulip form, typical of the 'Adam' period. This has a tapering cylinder rising from a circular base, with hollow flutes which increase the slender image, and continues on to the bell-shaped sconce above. Later, when Victorian makers covered their sticks with decoration, usually in large amounts and of every possible description, it is not always easy to see the basic form, but today, when most candlesticks are reproductions of the old, it is usually the plainer types that are copied, and Queen Anne is the favourite.

When more light was required candelabra were used and these were often made *en suite* as a set of candlesticks. They had branches which curved out in various ways from the top of the candle-holder, which was now filled in with the urn, flame, or other finial, to supply a socket for two, three or occasionally four candles. Candelabra, at their best in large, gracious rooms, were always taller than the candlesticks, sometimes enormously so, particularly during the nineteenth century. They are more easily faked, and harder to find in prime condition when they are very costly.

Of much greater interest to the collector is the chamberstick, taken by each individual to light himself to bed along dark corridors. These were made from the seventeenth century until they were no longer needed. They consisted of the sconce (the candle-holding part of a stick) as it would appear on the candlestick of the day, with a short stem (which became taller in the mid-eighteenth century), set on a plain round saucer, which in Queen Anne's time had fairly steep sides. They had a hollow handle, longer than those found later, when it became no more than a crook, with a thumbpiece on top. From about 1750 there was also a conical extinguisher, generally fitted on the inside of the handle, but sometimes on the sconce itself. Decoration consisted of a moulded border, gadrooning, or other simple motifs such as beading, husks, or in the early nineteenth century something more elaborate, surrounding the rim of the saucer, the extinguisher and the nozzle capping the sconce.

Superior examples also have snuffers lying on the saucer, which were undoubtedly originally made for most chambersticks and which, because they were totally separate, have seldom remained together. The snuffers and the stands or trays that accompanied were made prolifically, and although they do not survive in quantity, they can be collected. It is a strange fact that few candlesticks were made of silver in America, but things bearing English hallmarks, like snuffers, their trays and other objects, have crossed the Atlantic, to be searched out by the collector there.

Candles did not necessarily always burn evenly and well, as they do today, and one of the purposes of the scissor-like objects known as snuffers, was to trim the wick, pieces of which were collected up in the box soldered to the side of the longer blade. The oldest known pair of snuffers c. 1550, in the Victoria and Albert museum, London, has a heart-shaped box, engraved with the royal arms, an interesting inscription and very fine cast ornaments applied to the scissor blades. However, those appearing for sale are more likely to date from about 1700 to 1825. The stand is generally fairly simple, and is of baluster shape with applied mouldings, or perhaps gadrooned rims, with a base similar to those of contemporary candlesticks. Snuffers have usually been matched up as far as possible, but are rarely the originals. Any found to be by the same maker and in much the same style are acceptable. Snuffers generally had scrolling handles, engraved with a crest, the stems beaded, pierced, reeded, or quite plain, only nineteenth-century examples being chased all over with shells, scrolling, leafage, rosettes etc.

It cannot be certain that the snuffer tray was always intended as such, for they could have been used for other purposes, such as pens, while the stand, made at the same time, from the late seventeenth century, could not. They are, nevertheless, highly collectable. The Queen Anne variety are plain, on four bun feet, with a handle similar to those on chambersticks of the day. The waisted, hourglass shape came next, still on bun feet, or (later) shell feet, the border sometimes chased with flowers, scrolls or shells during the rococo period, although even then they could be very simple. The pierced gallery, a product of the modern age, but very attractive, appeared from about 1770, and the boat-shape, with gadrooned, beaded, or partly pierced borders, sometimes with down turned ends, arrived in about 1785. These pleasant trays have many uses today, and are really attractive.

But for those with even more limited space there is always the vesta box, an attractive trinket intended to hold the matches with which candles were lit. Like vinaigrettes these can be found in a great variety of forms, depicting objects such as books, flasks, wheatsheaves and so forth and were mostly made in Birmingham (although they are not always hall-marked) from the last quarter of the nineteenth century. They are often to be found in the back of a drawer with a jumble of items not considered worth displaying, and are worth rummaging for for they cost very little money and can be a lot of fun to collect.

TOP *a christening cup by Stuart Devlin with hand made gold figures, London, 1972*

RIGHT *a 24 light candelabrum with articulated candle holders by Stuart Devlin*

Tapersticks of 1710 and 1735 showing how little the form had changed in 25 years, and a bulbous brandy warmer with the handle set at right angles to the tiny lip

Silver about the House

TOILET SETS · MIRRORS · CASKETS · ROUND POTS · PATCH BOXES · TOOTH POWDER BOXES
TOOTH PICK CASES · BRUSHES · COMBS · SCENT BOTTLES · SOAP BOXES · EYE BATHS
MEDICINE BOTTLES · BUTTONS · BUCKLES · CLASPS · LOCKETS
SPURS · INKSTANDS · QUILL CASES · SEAL BOXES · SEALS · PENKNIVES · LETTER OPENERS
BUTTER KNIVES · BUTTON HOOKS · CARDCASES · THIMBLES · PIN CUSHIONS · SILK WINDERS
GLOVE MENDERS · BODKINS · DARNERS · TAPE MEASURES · SHAVING BOWLS · STIRRUP CUPS
TOBACCO BOXES · IRISH FREEDOM BOXES

The gold toilet set belonging to Charles II's Queen was worth £4,000 before 1700, which gives one some idea of the priceless value of even individual dressing-table items today. Complete sets, in which all the pieces were made at the same time, were rare, most sets having drawn on stock or been commissioned from several different makers. The value of individual items, therefore, is not affected when they are separated, as most now are. The size of a set varied, the famous Calverley service (1683) in the Victoria and Albert Museum, having only thirteen pieces of very highly embossed silver in the Dutch style, while a silver gilt set at Luton Hoo, Bedfordshire, by David Willaume (1698–1722), consisted of twenty-eight pieces, mostly decorated only with gadroon borders. The contents of this latter set are fairly typical of most other sets made between about 1670 and 1750. It comprises candlesticks and snuffers, brushes and trays, boxes of all sizes, for powders, patches, combs and other trinkets, a ewer, scent bottles, pin-cushions, and sometimes standing salvers. Most sets had a mirror, framed in silver, usually with armorials on

top and from about 1685 a gadrooned or fluted border, with foliage at the corners, *chinoiserie* or, later, something more imposing.

The larger boxes were called caskets and were usually rectangular and anything up to ten inches long, but there were also smaller boxes, perhaps three or four inches square, and little round pots, which contained pomades or other aids to beauty. During the Queen Anne period boxes had corners cut to create an octagonal shape. They were sometimes set on four feet and usually had moulded, concave edges. Well-engraved armorials or light *chinoiserie* decoration enhanced the magnificence of the patina that age and quality have given them. It is interesting that some twentieth-century reproductions, made in Britannia silver with all the old grace, lack only this glow of old age. Caskets or other boxes too large for snuff can be bought today. One example (1758), heavily embossed with flowers and foliage, illustrates how little the basic shape of the original had changed, with its cut corners and four scroll and bracket feet. The majority, however, that are to be found are nineteenth-century, heavily embossed, and generally Birmingham made. They are more useful than snuff boxes and can be very attractive, particularly the later ones in the style of *art nouveau*.

The round pomade pots, which were also used to hold glue, are most useful for face powder and have been reproduced freely, often in glass with a silver lid. Original examples do appear for sale but only

LEFT *an American three-handled cup by Tiffany and Co., New York, c 1898, showing how heavy decoration had become by the end of the century*

occasionally. Some may have been used to hold patches, as important then as lipstick is today, but the box made for the purpose, mostly during the late-seventeenth century, was much smaller. One large survivor from 1690 was sold recently—only one-and-a-half inches across, with a lift-off lid engraved with a tulip. In view of their size and age it is unlikely that many of the tiny silver containers kept in modern handbag or pocket for pills or sweeteners were originally patch boxes. They are more likely to be a vinaigrette with the delightful grille torn out or even a nutmeg grater similarly gutted.

The arrangement of patches on the face was more important than washing and a toothpowder box (Birmingham, 1795), which is decorated in bright cut, may have been before its time. Silver-backed brushes, used for clothes or beards, were included in many toilet sets (and made prolifically since) and a magnificent pair, c. 1785, appeared recently. Combs, used to hold the unkempt mass of hair in order in less salubrious days, were of the ornamental variety, the long teeth, like those in the nineteenth century, capped with workmanship of great delicacy. The scent bottle was a necessity at that time. Although those in the Luton Hoo set could be mistaken for Queen Anne caddies, octagonal with a dome on top, the majority seen for sale were made in the nineteenth century. They were often engraved with armorials or crests or took a gimmicky form, of objects such as bird's eggs or the bird itself. Some were of glass with silver mounts—tops and sometimes a base to hold the bottles—themselves varied and often very fine.

The *toilette* of these ladies has produced varied and fascinating items for collection including silver soap boxes, eye baths and medicine bottles. Collectable items associated with dressing may also be wider in range than would at first be imagined.

Variety in buttons (see Chapter I) is almost endless and the subject of at least one monthly magazine in America. Buckles, going through periods of high fashion, have been used to some extent at all times

LEFT *a coral and rattle by Joseph Willmore, Birmingham; 1812*

TOP RIGHT *an embossed box by John Lawrence and Co., Birmingham; 1826*
BELOW *is its mark*

RIGHT *this Queen Anne casket dated 1707 is particularly beautiful when seen due to the glow of age and the lovely colour of Britannia standard silver*

since the Romans, and are also incredibly varied. A look at any museum of fashion (such as the one in Bath, not far from the American Museum in England) will show how they were used on shoes, belts, knees etc., according to custom at the time. Great numbers of buckles were made in Birmingham from mid-Georgian days, and they were really varied in the 1890s when the style of embossing was naturalistic. The collector stands a real chance of making a find – in an old chest in the attic or at the back of a drawer – thereby creating the personal nucleus of a collection that can also include clasps. These were used for sashes, the elegant stocks worn by Victorian ladies, or as the lovely fasteners for necklaces. Two fine specimens appeared in a Boston exhibition in 1956, each engraved with an eagle on an oval shield.

During the Commonwealth (1649–60) the Royalist lady may well have worn a locket around her neck hidden under her clothes, bearing a portrait of Charles I, in memoriam, which she joyously changed to one of Charles II, in thanksgiving, when the monarchy was restored. But the heart-shaped locket around the neck of the ordinary lovelorn maiden would have been inscribed with words of undying love and contained a lock of her lover's hair and possibly his portrait. These attractive lockets continued to be made throughout the nineteenth century, similar in concept (though very different in price) to a 1620 example which was sold a few years ago. Love tokens have always been passed between young people and can be very regional in character, the Luckenbooth brooches, for instance, being peculiar to Scotland, particularly the north although they originated in Edinburgh. These small eighteenth-century brooches are often heart-shaped and some of the inscriptions are most touching. It is fascinating to discover who the couples were and then to trace their subsequent histories in parish registers, a pastime open free to anyone interested in romantic history in any of its many forms.

Before going out horseback riding the lady would fix on her spurs, which fitted tightly around her dainty foot. They were too light to be effective, and although most had a spiked wheel it was hardly capable of even tickling the horse. Spurs are quite collectable and look very pretty on a shelf. Like those intended only for ceremonial wear by men, they were made in London originally and Birmingham later, and were all fully hallmarked.

Such a lady could probably write and the fine quality of the inkstand, called a standish until about 1800, shows the importance of this skill. These stands, basically lovely trays on four feet, contained all that

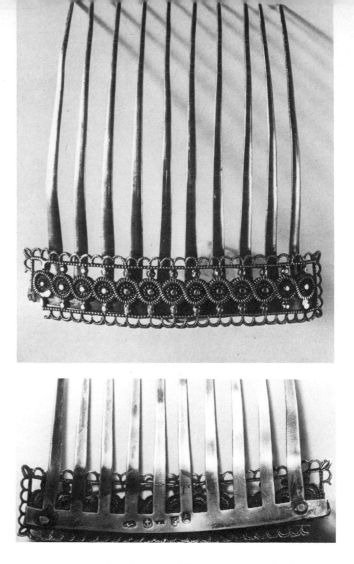

was necessary for the art of letter writing before the days of fountain pens, when the writer might take up her quill (although gold or silver pens were known), check that it was sharp enough, dip it into the inkwell (one item common to all inkstands) and start to write. But then some fine powder (called pounce) or sand had to be shaken on to the page from the box provided, to prevent the ink from running berserk on the un-sized paper. When finished, the letter was put into an ungummed envelope, a taper lit and a wafer taken from its place in the inkstand, the wax heated and the flap closed with the lady's personal seal. The finest inkstands also include a bell, which would otherwise stand separately on her table, so that a servant could be summoned to take the letter.

Originally and until about 1730 in England, these stands were in the form of a box with four bun feet and a hinged lid, and were known as 'Treasury' inkstands. They are not really collectable but were well reproduced from the last part of the nineteenth century. In Boston, John Coney (who died in 1722) made an inkstand of the type that was general later, with the important difference being that his was triangular. It has cut corners, a plain moulded rim,

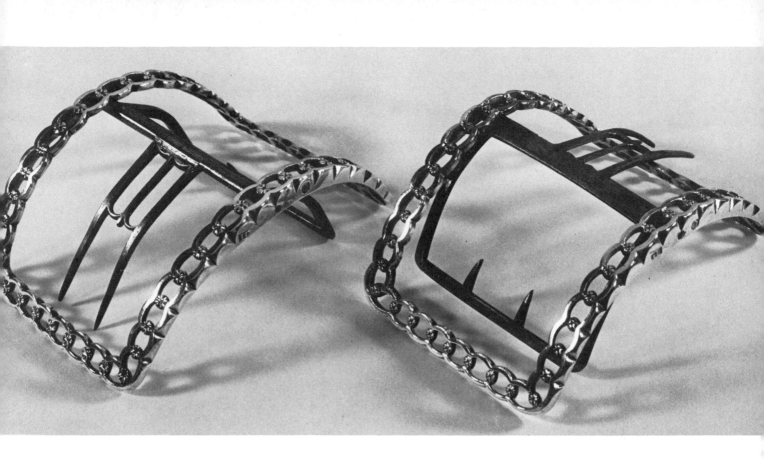

three fine lion couchant feet, and is in the Metropolitan Museum of Art, New York. It can be carried by means of a ring handle on a baluster stem in the centre which is surrounded by three round Queen Anne style boxes, one (with pierced cover inset) for sand, one for pounce and the other for ink. It is elegant and truly outstanding. The Victoria and Albert Museum, London, has a beautiful example (1729) by Paul de Lamerie. The conventional stand is more like a salver, with a lovely scroll and shell edge. This has only two pots showing, with a bell standing over a well for seals, an accessory that increases the value greatly. Pots and bell were arranged similarly in a rope-edged example of 1753, sold in New York recently, but by this time a groove for pens had been added in front. This groove is also seen on another (1745) by Paul de Lamerie (sold in London) which has lovely scrolling decoration and is set on four finely cast lion's-paw feet. It has two silver-topped glass bottles (quite usual—particularly later) and a taperstick. Even lovelier is an example of 1741 which has an oval tray on four scroll and foliage feet, ribbed like a strawberry dish but surrounded by a gorgeous shell rim, with three beautifully shaped pots, the centre

one surmounted by a candle-holder. Inkstands appear for sale quite frequently dated from about 1750 and to me any idea that the stand could have once been a snuffer tray, as frequently suggested, is incorrect, the shape in most cases being quite different. If therefore, it looks like a snuffer tray and lacks sockets for its various pots, or depression for pens, examine its marks carefully, comparing them to those on all its other separate pieces; this will give a positive answer. Styles of ornamentation followed those of the times, but from about 1755 pierced galleries sometimes surrounded the stand like a fence, also forming inside divisions, although low pierced frames for the pots on a footed tray with a pen depression in front, is more usual. They could be very large during the nineteenth century, not out of place on a heavy Victorian writing-table, but many retained the simple form even then, and particularly in Ireland. They had gadroon, rope or shell borders, and the addition of an extinguisher to the chamber type of taperstick and sometimes a seal box as well.

There were many other items connected with writing that did not always have a place on the ink stand, including a quill case, which could, on a

The top and underside of a seal by Charles Hancock, Birmingham; c 1808

sophisticated model, incorporate a seal on its base. A seal box is one of the most enigmatic objects, as any box of sufficient size could have served this purpose. There was no doubt, however, about one round box (1832) which was nearly seven inches in diameter, with a hinged lid stamped with the royal arms, for this contained a wax impression of the great seal of William IV. The seal itself was extremely prolific in its day and even the public scribe, writing letters for the illiterate, used one. These sometimes bore initials, a crest or even arms, particularly when belonging to a livery company, college or civic dignitary, for the majority of provincial town hallmarks were taken from the arms of the borough, as found on its civic seal or mayorial chains.

A penknife was used, as its name implies, to sharpen the quill and enough of these were of silver to create a good subject for collection, and during the *art nouveau* period they were decorated most charmingly. The form lent itself even better to the longer shape of letter openers, which were very common at that time. Today, when gum is stronger than in 1900, Georgian skewers, particularly those for game, are used for this purpose, but butter knives also do the job well. These were made from about 1800 and usually had a flat-shaped blade, not unlike a Victorian fish server, decorated on the blade with bright cut, flat chasing or engraving, never in excess. They can be most attractive, particularly in shape, the earlier ones having bone, ivory or wooden handles, while those that came later were usually all silver with the handle taking any of the conventional spoon patterns described in the next chapter and with less decoration on the blade as a rule. Other items, such as individual ink-pots, travelling inkwells, rulers, pens or silver mounted blotters, may also be found to add to a collection of writing materials.

When the lady went calling, fastening her silk gloves with the help of a silver button hook designed for this delicate purpose, her personal calling cards were kept clean in a silver card case. The cards were presented to the lady being visited on a silver salver by her servant or, if she were not at home, left on the salver in the hall. A few cases took these cards length-wise, the majority upright, with a lid fitting closely over an interior sleeve. They were made wherever goldsmiths worked in Victorian times, particularly in Birmingham (where Nathaniel Mills gave them his usual stately home treatment) and New York. Usually highly embossed, often with delightful scenes, they are quite easy to find. They are of wide variety and great interest, and are useful for credit cards today.

The art of the needlewoman, like most of her imple-

ABOVE *three presentation pieces, a salver, cup and water pitcher by Francis W Cooper, New York; 1860*

BELOW *a bottle top by Samuel Bakes, Birmingham; 1787*

ments, had been known for thousands of years, and many accessories, such as pin-cushions, scissors, bodkins and silk-winders are collectable and date from the start of the seventeenth century. Thimbles, made in their millions in many materials, including gold and silver (although, because of size, few survive before the nineteenth century), are surprisingly varied and the subject of at least one entire book in America. In most cases variety is achieved in a decorative frieze around the open end, the working part covered in the usual stipple, or occasionally, other indented forms. The frieze, embossed, or engraved, could consist of a pretty, decorative border commemorating a battle, a life or other historical event. Sometimes just a holiday place, the letters of MARGATE, for example, in high relief, formed the decoration. Others may have a shield attached to the side, above the frieze with initials, or even a crest, while really superior models have precious stones inset, even diamonds on occasion, either enriching the frieze or forming a design, such as a flower, on the side.

Needlecases found from Stuart times, are only rarely of silver, and hardly collectable. Pin-cushions, however, once a part of those lovely toilet sets, have been made ever since that time. The designs changed with the times but not the overall concept of stuffed

material into which pins can be stuck, surrounded by silver in almost any imaginable shape. Pots of all sorts, with or without handles were favourites, but models of horses, even camels, with a cushioned saddle, a tortoise or other animals with soft tops, are known. The oldest examples had a moulded border, with foliage, petalled or geometric, overlapping the base of the cushion, and some were made to tie on the needle-woman's wrist for convenience when sewing a hem.

Other items that could find their way into a collection of small sewing accessories, are silk-winders (a necessity in the days before cotton reels), glove menders, which had a long, slim length of silver, decorated in many ways, between two ebony, bone or enamelled tips of differing sizes to insert into a glove finger; bodkins, darners (the egg, again at the end of a decorated silver handle, sometimes combining with a glove mender) and tape measures, which are very varied in decoration when round, but may also be found spewing forth tape from the mouth of a fish, or other animal. Scissors would also form a major part of such a collection, varied as they are both in style and purpose, if it were not that they were so rarely made in silver. Some of these objects can be found from very early times, but all of them were made at least until the turn of this century, often becoming more fanciful as time went by.

Things used by the man of the household do not compare when it comes to collecting, for little that he did needed suitable objects for the purpose. Some magnificent Queen Anne shaving bowls can be seen in museums, plain with a moulded rim and with a deep indent for the chin, while shaving brushes may be silver mounted. Hunting provides an enormous subject for specialized button collection, but stirrup cups go to those with a longer purse. These were the cups that cheer, passed at a meet, to those already mounted and waiting for the rest of the hunt to assemble. After 1760, these cups take the form of a fox's head. Whatever the contents (today it is usually port or cherry brandy . . . in glasses) the gentleman drank it and handed the cup back to the servant. The earliest of these fox-head cups had a very long, unrealistic face, later ones being cast in a much truer mould, but they were never made in quantity, a glass or silver goblet having been passed more often.

The collector of anything connected with smoking rarely confines himself to silver, for although pipes

130

and tampers were made in that metal, they are not usual. Smoking was quite a ritual, the gentlemen sitting down at leisure to enjoy it together. Because two hands were available the lid of tobacco boxes lifted off, but they are not as varied in decoration as those for snuff, and are enormously less common. Most of them are oval shape, about three-and-a-half to four-and-a-half inches wide, decorated with engraved arms, *repoussé* in the case of seventeenth-century examples. Few made in England were later than 1750, but Continental tobacco boxes, totally different, were made later.

The Irish Freedom Box (*c.* 1750–1850) was not unlike these, except that the shape varies. It can be oval, octagonal, escutcheon or most commonly circular. These boxes were a trifle smaller, averaging three inches and most bore an inscription describing the deed, or service, for which the Freedom of the city was bestowed, along with the arms of that city – Cork in a surprising number of cases. The most interesting feature of these boxes is the story behind them and they were treasured for generations by a family before the necessity to sell arose which gave the collector the opportunity to care for them in turn.

LEFT *24 buttons with different sporting motifs; c 1775*

ABOVE *a fine galleried inkstand by Kelward Aldridge, London; 1771*

BELOW *a George II small, plain oblong inkstand; 1727*

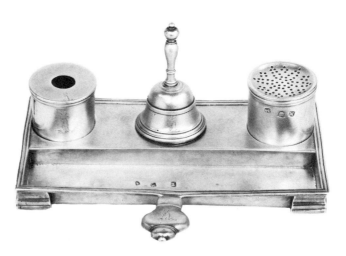

Spoons

The spoon is so wide a subject in scope that it caters for every depth of pocket and all shades of interest. The majority of spoons made in England before about 1600, which have survived, are in museums or the hands of great specialist collectors, but seventeenth-century spoons appear for sale quite frequently. Three enormous volumes have been written on the subject of English and Scottish spoons made before 1700, describing their workmanship, marks, and ambiguities in accurate and technical detail. Experts have compiled catalogues that clarify the subject still further, ascribing rare provincial marks in the light of new research, and dividing types of spoons into further sub-divisions, helpful to the researcher in depth.

Catalogues are also of great help to the collector of American spoons, for their classification is totally different, and spoons made during the last 150 years in thousands of different styles are largely traceable by pattern numbers, often given in addition to a mark, or by series of marks that denote the manufacturing company. An example with more marks than many is the Gorham Manufacturing Company which stamp a lion passant, an anchor and a large letter G in a shield. This silver, made by Gorham since 1831, can be dated accurately by differences in the lion; but they also used a date letter, in the English fashion, for a period. The majority of American spoons were made of coin silver, and when they were of sterling the fact was proclaimed. Sterling was used for all English silver and often pieces were of a higher standard. The Gorham Company adopted the sterling standard

for all its work in 1868, and thereafter the words 'Trade Mark' appear above the anchor, and 'sterling' below, with the style number, to be found in a given catalogue, incised also near the mark. Advertisers searching for spoons may, and frequently do, simply give a series of numbers, but others specify styles, such as 'Large Gorham Apostle Spoons', modelled in the style of English, or earlier still, 'Continental Apostle Spoons'.

It is not possible here to go into the intricacies of all types of American spoon; books have been written on most of them, since there are variations within each type. Figural spoons, for instance, depict many different Geisha girls, animals, Indians, cowboys and a host of other unspecified subjects; Christmas spoons are all slightly different; Fairy Tale spoons may be unlimited in their interpretation, while historical spoons (taken together with commemorative spoons), record almost every detail of American life, with scenes or figures engraved or embossed on the bowl of the spoon, its stem and terminal. Presentation spoons add thousands yearly to the supply, while eating spoons as made for the normal dinner service were produced by all the silver companies in the country who each continued to introduce different patterns until something really popular was found. Full sets of these, and especially spoons made by Tiffany and Company, are keenly bid for in the sale rooms of New York.

In addition to the enormous number of different types of American spoons, there are also regional characteristics, such as twisted stems of San Francisco, to be taken into account, and the identification of spoons, their maker, date, place and purpose is consequently difficult. It is further complicated by the amount of silver to be found of South American, Canadian or European origin, in addition to the quantities imported from England, Scotland and Ireland.

TOP LEFT *two of a set of six trifid teaspoons with typical foliate engraving; c 1670.* RIGHT *a pair of silver-gilt sugar sifters with pierced and crested shell back bowls and scroll terminals, c 1740.* BELOW *two sauce ladles by Paul de Lamerie having the Onslow pattern, c 1740*

The fascination of old English spoons lies, to a large extent, in their great antiquity, their history unfolding with that of England and its people. No other object has survived in such quantities although fourteenth- and fifteenth-century spoons belong to museums. These include the diamond point with its very thin stem, the acorn top, the wrythen knop which has a spiral flame finial, and the moor's head. However the keen collector can buy sixteenth-century spoons if blessed with an understanding bank manager and good luck. Spoons with other finials were also made very early, for example the Buddha knopped spoon which was a Devonshire speciality, and the Maidenhead spoon, which is one that is most frequently found, has the head of a girl, full face, with her long hair flowing down her back. It was made from the fourteenth century, and like all spoons it was gilded, or partially gilded.

The lion sejant, seal top and Apostle spoon are also very early, and although the lion (c. 1500–1620, and later in the provinces), sitting on his plinth at the spoon top belongs to museums, the seal top and Apostle (c. 1450–1650) can be collected. All spoons from about 1485 have their terminal set on a thick, hexagonal stem, tapering very slightly towards the top, with a broader surface back and front. The bowl is fig- or pear-shaped, those on the earliest spoons being more elongated than later examples, although the change was very gradual. All have the leopard's head or provincial town mark stamped in the bowl of the spoon near the stem, and have the date letter, lion passant and maker's mark on the back of the stem fairly near the base, when they are correctly marked (this does not apply to the slipped end spoon). Provincial makers, however, very often stamped their own mark (initials or a device) three times instead of stamping a full set, and they also stamped some extraordinary variations which have kept the experts guessing ever since. Nothing else can provide such a rich source of unascribed marks, the unravelling of which has been the subject of deep research in recent years. This has changed the picture regularly, and has made the oldest books on marks of little value, and even Jackson unreliable, unless revised annually with newly proved ascriptions included.

The seal top spoon, made during the same period as the lion sejant, survives in the greatest quantity and can be bought more easily. The bowl was large compared to the length of stem in the early days, and like all spoons that were constantly used, the left side is frequently worn considerably thinner than the right which should be thick, with a good edge. Worn

examples are shunned by the purist, but nevertheless, appear more personal. The seal top, a flat circle rarely, if ever, bearing a seal (although initials are usual), completes a baluster finial that may be tooled in a variety of ways. The manner in which a finial is joined to the stem must be examined, for no genuine spoon is cast in one piece, a 'V' splice being normal in London, while provincial makers usually used a method reminiscent of a cabinet maker's dovetail joint, seen more easily from the side. This applies to all spoons of the period, which also tend to become lighter and less substantial from about 1600.

The great early favourite was the Apostle spoon, made for two hundred years and faked or copied ever since. A full set, of which only three or four survive intact, consisted of thirteen spoons, the twelve

BELOW *detail of the finial of the centre spoon opposite.*

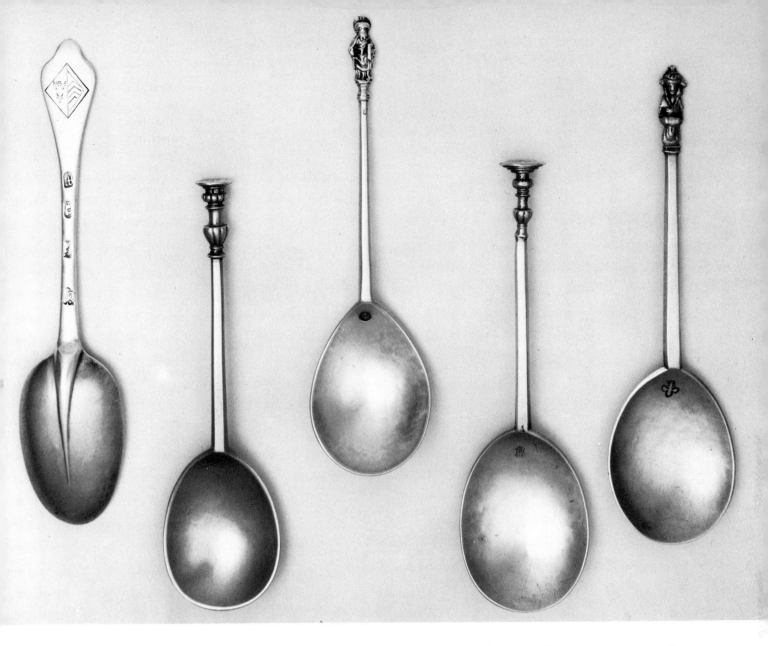

ABOVE *left to right, a dog nose table spoon with rat tail bowl by Henry Greene 1701; an Elizabeth I silver-gilt seal top spoon 1562; a Henry VII Apostle spoon, possibly St Bartholomew, 1490; a Charles I seal top spoon, by Arthur Hazlewood, Norwich, 1638; a Buddha knopped spoon, west country, 1630*

FOLLOWING PAGE: *left, part of an American service of flatware, Gorham Co.; c 1900. The handles are elaborately chased and there are over 220 pieces. right, four Charles I Apostle spoons, London; 1629. Notice the lovely thick edges to spoons of this date*

Apostles, each carrying his own symbol of martyrdom, and the Master spoon showing the figure of Christ holding the Orb and Cross. The majority of these spoons were made singly, often to the order of a godparent for a child's christening, perhaps four going to the lucky few whose godfathers could afford it. Collectors enjoy matching up a set, collecting twelve Apostles of similar quality, made by the same maker, or in the same year, but it is unlikely that any will prove to have been made as a set. The finest full set in the world can be seen in the Huntington Art Gallery, San Marino, California, made in 1527 by a London goldsmith who stamped his work (to be seen in many English and American museums) with a fringed 'S'. Few ever achieved the precision of his tooling but it is a mistake to think that the work of provincial spoon makers was necessarily inferior to those of London. Nevertheless, collecting different provincial marks is a popular method of specializing, as is the collecting of unusual spoons of good quality and in good condition. This is important, since inferiority or damage can sometimes be mistaken for a

Two of a set of six Elizabeth I silver-gilt lion-sejant spoons; RIGHT *is a detail of one of the lions*

him off after stoning, St Thomas has a spear, St Matthew and St Bartholomew both carry a flaying knife, having been flayed alive, but St Matthew is also found with a wallet, since he was a tax gatherer, St Matthias has an axe, St John a cup and an eagle, St Simon Zelotes a saw, St Philip and St Jude the tall crosses on which they were crucified, though St Jude also carries a carpenter's square and St Philip a staff. St Peter carries the Keys to the Kingdom of Heaven, and they all also hold a book, cast as part of the figure, as is the nimbus, or halo, on their heads. This might be pierced between 1520 and 1580, or show a dove in relief on the upper surface after 1600, depicting the Holy Ghost descending upon them. The halo on the earliest spoons is worn rather on the back of the head, like a schoolboy's cap, while those made later wore theirs very straight, as obviously a good saint should. Few subjects can be more full of interest.

The earliest type of English spoon also to be made in America was the slip end, a beautifully proportioned plain spoon made in England between about 1475 and 1660. This has the normal hexagonal stem (square in America), slightly broader at the top, making a good thickness for the oblique cut that finishes the spoon, and for the date letter stamped high on its back. This spoon is not the same as the Puritan, although both lack a finial, for the latter spoon, made prolifically in Boston, is cut square on top and is the first type to have a flat stem tapering towards the bowl. In England they appeared during the middle years of the century. Their thick stems, masculine in their austerity, were later hammered out to create a broad, flat end that took a very feminine trefoil shape after the Restoration and they became known as trifid spoons.

This was the start of a whole new era. The bowl of the spoon, previously at its most narrow where the stem joins, now became a symmetrical oval, soon after becoming longer and more narrow at the tip, at times even pointed, particularly in Scotland and Ireland. Marks were spaced evenly up the back of the flat stem, the front of which was sometimes flat chased or engraved, while the back of the bowl might also have a stamped or cast scrolling pattern known as a lacy back. Whether plain or decorated, virtually all trifids have a long tapering rib running down the back of the bowl known as a rat-tail, a feature that continued in use until after 1730 and although such spoons might have a different top, such as a dog-nose, they are always referred to as rat-tail spoons.

John Coney made one of the most perfect trifids to be seen, and it is amongst a fine collection of American spoons in the Yale University Art Gallery, Connecti-

new or unusual pattern. The symbol carried by each Apostle was cast separately, and these are easily broken off, giving an altogether wrong impression when replaced later. Beware of the spoon that has been regilded for it may hide repairs.

In theory each Apostle should be recognized by the symbol he carries, but in fact there are variations making this difficult, while the finial, cast in an old mould that had lost definition originally, may be so rubbed that it cannot be identified. Some of the symbols found include St James the Greater, with his pilgrim's staff and his hat slung across his back, symbolic of his pilgrimage to Spain; St James the Lesser, with the fuller's bat that was used to finish

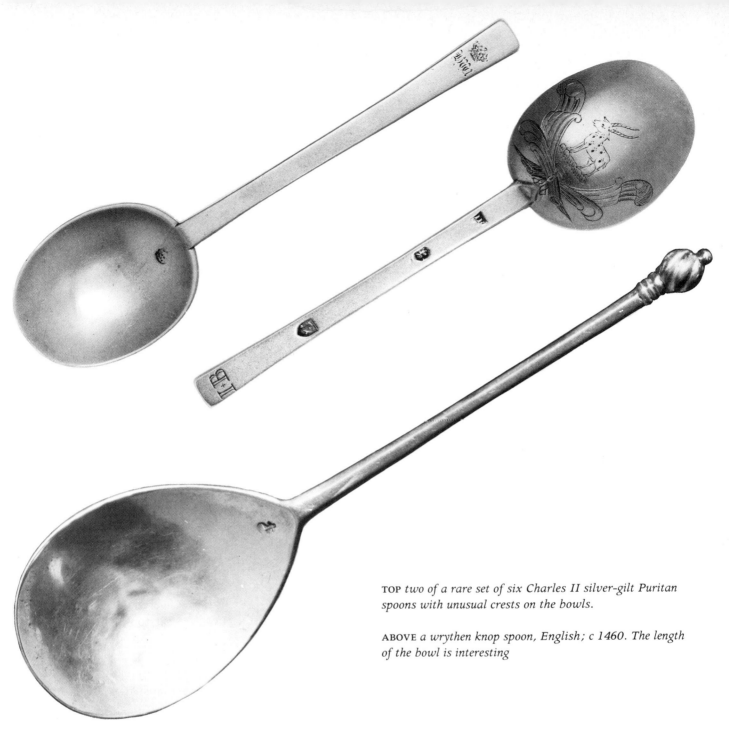

TOP *two of a rare set of six Charles II silver-gilt Puritan spoons with unusual crests on the bowls.*

ABOVE *a wrythen knop spoon, English; c 1460. The length of the bowl is interesting*

cut. At the same time (*c.* 1680–1700) New York goldsmiths were making spoons in the Dutch style, with a heavy scrolled stem and a mournful terminal, to present to pall bearers after a funeral. Not many survive. American spoons after this were fairly conventional with a few outstanding examples, until, towards the end of the eighteenth century, a very pretty fluted bowl was used, pointed at the tip; the curved handle with a shoulder just above the joint was enriched with bright cut engraving. The drop (i.e. rat-tail) on the back of the bowl took fanciful forms (as they had in England somewhat earlier) such as shell, leaf or a dove, and soon after 1800 the coffin-end spoon appeared, a totally American form,

the squared cut corners at its end looking exactly like a coffin.

Towards the end of the century forks, first used after the Restoration in England, became more usual. Although rare, late-seventeenth-century examples have even appeared for sale recently, with two, sometimes three prongs, good trifid ends, and a fine set of marks evenly spaced up their backs. The 'trifid' period also introduced spoons of varying sizes, the small teaspoon, the normal sized dessert spoon and the large table spoon. From now on the service of cutlery developed, and although a complete canteen from before 1800 is difficult to buy it is possible, by diligent search, to build up a good set in a given pattern

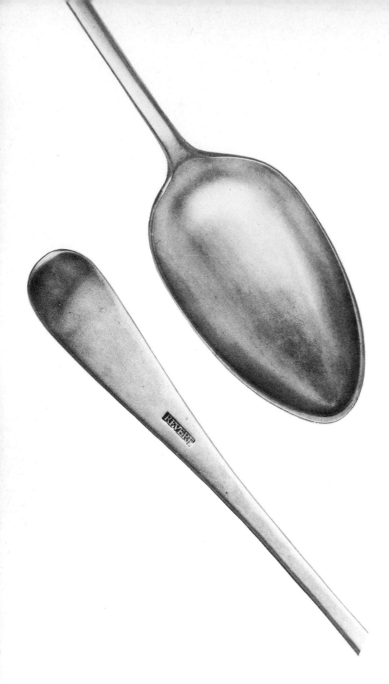

ABOVE *tablespoons by Paul Revere, Boston; 1796*

RIGHT *part of an Empire silver-gilt dessert service by François Dominique Nandin, Paris; c 1810. The piercing on the sugar sifter is typical of French work*

of the work of one maker, or of one date, if not both.

The dog-nose spoon, so like the trifid but without the notches, lasted until roughly 1714 when a round-ended spoon handle, known as Hanoverian, appeared. This style lasted until 1770, characterized by a ridge which ran down the front of the handle from the rounded, upturned tip and usually petered out about half way. The back of the bowl featured a good rat-tail until after 1735, when a short, round, rather dull drop took its place. It could also have the slightly

more interesting double drop, with one tongue over-lapping the other. There was little variation on this theme over the years except for the picture backs that first appeared, mostly on teaspoons, around the middle of the eighteenth century. These could consist of arms but were more often pictorial, sometimes commemorative but very often with political implications. The study of them can turn into a great hobby, with far more involved than just collecting the spoons.

The Onslow patterned spoon (*c.* 1745–60) was made during the Hanoverian period, and had a broad scroll end, which curved away backwards, its ridges tapering off on the front of the stem itself. This rare, striking style looks particularly well on ladles, with their fluted bowls. The Old English pattern took over in about 1770, designed, for the first time, to be laid face upwards on the table, so shifting interest from the back to the front of the spoon. The tip therefore bends slightly back, the handle becomes somewhat convex, and a ridge runs down the back, reversing the form of the Hanoverian, while decoration on the stem front becomes normal. At first (1765–85) this decoration was beautifully simple, designed to accentuate the shape of the spoon itself. This was achieved by such means as feather edging, diagonal cuts like the spines of a feather which were also found on late-Hanoverian spoons, but never used after 1780 unless added out of period; the threaded edge, outlining the spoon, the beaded edge, seen less often, and the hesitant wriggle edge. When bright cut engraving came in, this covered the stem and became the focus of interest.

The well-named fiddle pattern appeared with the new century and has been popular ever since. This has a broad end, narrowing sharply (less so in America where it sometimes almost tapers) to a narrow stem, with tiny wings just above the bowl. This spoon was frequently left plain, but the threaded edge was usual, to which a shell was added at the top when Regency taste demanded heavy ornament. To this, for good measure, they added heavy ornament on both sides of the stem, and classical stylized scrolls and called it King's pattern. Queen's pattern, seen less often, was the same without the shells, giving an altogether different appearance. By this time every size and shape of spoon, fork, ladle and server was being made in any chosen pattern. The forks now had four prongs, as they had had occasionally since 1750, although three appear to have been much more usual.

The patterns described above are the standard styles for English cutlery, to be found with only small modifications whatever the form and degree of decoration that may have been used since.

Acknowledgements

The publishers would like to thank the following organizations and individuals for their kind permission to reproduce the pictures in this book:

Antique Dealer and Collector's Guide:
  courtesy of Nottingham Castle Museum, Gibbs Collection, 22 top, 63.
  courtesy of S J Phillips, London, 87.
  courtesy of S J Shrubsole, 18 bottom, 19.

Birmingham Assay Office, 37, 47, 52, 64 bottom, 124, 125 top, 126, 127, 128, 129 bottom.

Christie, Manson and Woods, London, 58 top, 61 bottom, 79 top, 81, 103, 108, 125 bottom, 131 bottom, 138, 139 top, 141.

Collingwood of Conduit Street Ltd, London, 119.

Firestone and Parson, Boston, 99.

Thomas Lumley Ltd, 11, 18 top, 55, 71 top right, 72–73, 92, 102 bottom, 114, 131 top.

Louis Wine Ltd, 53, 67.

Metropolitan Museum of Art, New York:
  Bequest of A T Clearwater (1933), 6–7, 94.
  Fletcher Fund (1959), 62 bottom.
  Samuel D Lee Fund (1938), 46.
  Bequest of Charles Allen Mann (1924), 110.
  Rogers Fund, 1946, 29 bottom.

Museum of Fine Arts, Boston, Mass., 23, 27, 30 top and bottom, 31, 54 bottom, 58 top, 82, 91, 95, 98 top and bottom.
  Bequest of Charles Hitchcock Tyler, 50.

Octopus Books Ltd:
  courtesy of Collingwood of Conduit Street Ltd, London, jacket, endpapers, 2–3, 106–107.
  courtesy of Victoria and Albert Museum, London, (photographed by A C Cooper) 15, 26, 54 top, 86, 90.

Parke-Bernet Galleries, New York, 4, 8, 10, 16 top and bottom, 20 top and bottom, 21 bottom, 28, 32, 33, 35, 36, 40–41, 45 bottom, 53, 62 top, 66, 70, 74, 76, 78, 79 bottom, 80, 84, 85, 88, 89, 93, 101, 109, 112, 115, 122, 129 top, 136, 140.

S J Shrubsole, London, 83.

Sotheby and Co, London, 21 top, 24–25, 29 top, 34, 38, 39, 42, 44, 45 top, 48, 49, 56–57, 60, 61 top, 64 top, 65, 68, 71 left, 75, 77, 79 centre, 96, 100, 104–105, 113, 116, 117, 120–121, 130, 132, 134–135, 137.

Spink and Son Ltd, London, 139 bottom.

Woburn Abbey Collection, by kind permission of His Grace, the Duke of Bedford, 51, 59, 102 top.

Index

144